The Net-Works

Searching the Internet

Learn how to attract visitors to your site and keep them coming back for more!

Mark Neely

NET-WORKS
PO BOX 200
Harrogate
HG1 2YR
England

www.net-works.co.uk
Email: sales@net-works.co.uk
Fax: +44 (0) 1423 526035

Net.Works is an imprint of Take That Ltd.

Published in association with Maximedia Pty Ltd. (A.C.N. 002 666 579), PO Box 529, Kiama, NSW 2533, Australia.

ISBN: 1-873668-86-4

Text Copyright ©2000 Mark Neely & Maximedia Pty Ltd.
Design & Layout Copyright © 2000 Take That Ltd

All rights reserved around the world. This publication is copyright and may not be reproduced, in whole or in part, in any manner (except for excerpts thereof for bona fide purposes in accordance with the Copyright Act) without the prior consent in writing from the Publisher.

10 9 8 7 6 5 4 3 2 1

Trademarks:
Trademarked names are used throughout this book. Rather than place a trademark symbol in every occurance of a trademark name, the names are being used only in an editorial fashion for the benefit of the trademark owner, with no intention to infringe the trademark.

Printed and bound in The United Kingdom.

Disclaimer:
The information in this publication is distributed on an "as is" basis, without warranty. While very effort has been made to ensure that this book is free from errors or omissions, neither the author, the publisher, or their respective employees and agents, shall have any liability to any person or entity with respect to any liability, loss or damage caused or alleged to have been caused directly or indirectly by advice or instructions contained in this book or by the computer hardware or software products described herein. **Readers are urged to seek prior expert advice before making decisions, or refraining from making decisions, based on information or advice contained in this book.**

TTL books are available at special quantity discounts to use as premiums and sales promotions. For more information, please contact the Director of Special Sales at the above address or contact your local bookshop.

Contents

Preface 5

1. Searching the Net 7

2. What is the WWW? .10

3. The Virtual Library .16

4. The Information Chase 19

5. The Anatomy of a Search Engine 27

6. Information Retrieval Concepts 33

7. Yahoo! 37

8. AltaVista 43

9. Looksmart 55

10. Lycos 58

11. GO.com 63

12. A New Generation 68

13. Meta-Search Engines 73

continued

The Net-Works Guide to...

14. Finding Someone Online *80*

15. Other Research Options *85*

16. In Search of the Future *97*

Appendix: Search Engines and Software *103*

Glossary *106*

Preface

The history of Internet Search Engines, short though it is, is very interesting.
In the Web's formative years, Search Engines were extremely basic. In fact, they consisted of little more than long lists of Web sites that the Engine's creator found interesting. One of the oldest and best known Search Engines, Yahoo!, started out in this fashion.

As the lists of interesting Web sites grew, Search Engines began presenting information in different formats - including alphabetised lists, categories and subcategories - to make it easier to find specific sites within the list.

The first rudimentary search interfaces generally limited searches to matching words in the URL (Uniform Resource Locator) or title of a Web site. Later interfaces paired Web sites and detailed summaries of their contents in a searchable database.

The popularity of Search Engines grew in tandem with the Web's popularity. As hundreds of new Web sites sprang up each day, users found it increasingly difficult to keep track of them all. Search Engines became essential tools to find specific sites and information on the Web. Search Engines became the first port of call when searching for information or, in the case of a particularly complex search, several Search Engines were used to together find sites from where you could start your journey.

It soon became apparent that no single Search Engine could offer a definitive guide to the contents of the Web. This led to the creation of Meta-Search Engines - search interfaces that submit a query to multiple Search Engines at once and then collate the collective responses.

As the popularity of Search Engines grew, entrepreneurs decided they should transform to become "portals". Portals were intended to be the ultimate Web destination, offering news, sports, weather, online games and chats, free home page hosting, email accounts, horoscopes and more. Billions of dollars were spent in an attempt to generate user friendly, useful content and services that would attract millions of visitors.

Meanwhile, portals became increasingly useless as a reference point for finding new Web sites. In addition, the search process was becoming corrupted as portals allowed advertisers to buy a place in search results for their Web site or advert. Users could no longer tell the difference between relevant and useful links and paid results.

Web users revolted. Some launched or joined mailing lists that offered regular (usually daily) announcements of new sites. Others created Web directories listing sites of specific interest to certain groups of users, such as doctors, accountants, parents and mechanics. Still others joined online communities where members could post Web site recommendations and read reviews of sites.

These defections led to the launch of a new generation of "no frills" Search Engines, such as Google. These Search Engines don't offer special content, games or email accounts. Instead, they provide powerful, user-friendly search interfaces. You'll find out more about these later in the book.

Google's growing popularity has forced several established portals to rethink their strategies. As this book was being written, a major portal - AltaVista -launched its own separate, search-only service: Raging Search. No doubt other portals will follow.

The current trend away from top-heavy content sites and the focus on providing relevant, speedy and useful search services will undoubtedly benefit Web users.

And that's a good thing.

Mark Neely,

May 2000

Introduction

Searching the Net

It's easy to see why the World Wide Web has attracted so much attention in recent years.
Not since the advent of the printing press has humankind wielded such a powerful communications tool. Almost overnight, it seems, we have been given unlimited access to a global electronic publishing medium that - unlike earlier forms of mass communication - is open to everyone. Using the Web individuals and corporations alike can make information available to the masses.

The World Wide Web has been heralded as a boon for educational and research communities, as it provides efficient and cost-effective access to many information sources around the globe. Today, it's also transforming the way societies around the world view and consume entertainment. Made-for-the-Web movies and Internet-only books are online, and popular TV shows and magazines run Web sites where viewers and readers can interact with their favourite media personalities.

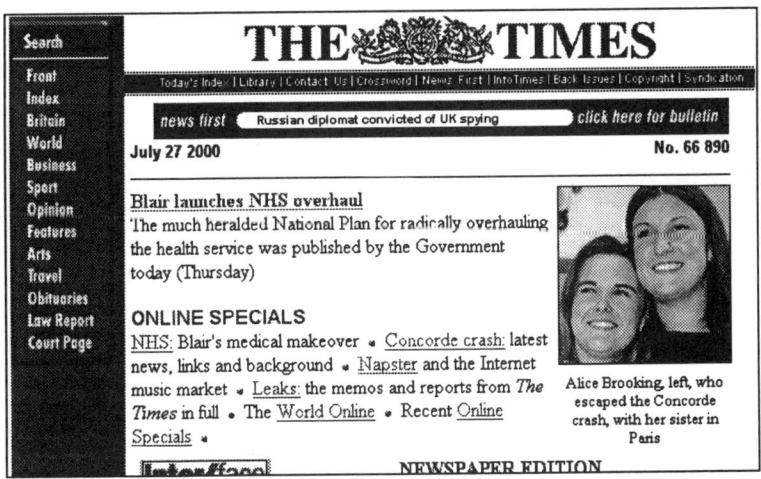

Your daily 'paper' - www.thetimes.co.uk

The Changing Face of Information Dissemination

The Web offers access to up-to-the-minute news, weather information, sports results, editorial and opinion columns, articles and research papers - even entire encyclopaedias are available online. Library catalogues, index systems, government databases and public records are rapidly making the transition from paper to electronic storage. In short, access to any public information service is now as close as your PC.

It's all there - and most of it is available free or at minimal cost.

Yet the staggering volume of information available online and the unprecedented growth of the Internet's information resources have the potential to cripple this medium before its power can be realised.

The Information Challenge

The scope of information available online is mind-boggling. In addition, because it has been collected and distributed in a non-structured manner and presented in many different formats, attempts to locate information can be frustratingly fruitless - unless you are adept at finding your way around the Web.

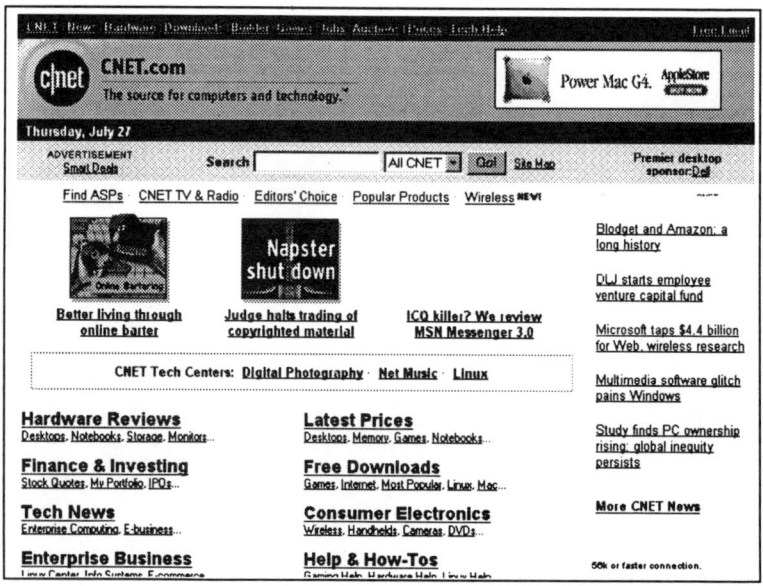

Beating the Information Blues

This book is designed primarily to teach readers to use the Web and its many search tools efficiently.

It will introduce readers to principles that guide information gathering on the Web, as well as focusing on search tools that enhance productivity and efficiency. The vast amount of information generated each day via Usenet (Internet news) and email mailing lists will also be examined, including how you can tap into these to find the material you want.

How to Use This Book

This book aims to teach readers how to use the Internet as a research tool, with particular emphasis on Search Engines. It is not designed as a thorough introduction to the principles of networking, specific Internet resources or the Internet in general. Instead, it is aimed at those who already have some experience using the Internet and the World Wide Web, and wish to hone their Internet research skills.

In writing this book and preparing the examples and screen shots, I have focused mainly on Windows-based software. However, the general principles outlined are applicable to all Internet users, whether accessing via Macintosh or Windows-based PCs - or any other flavours in between.

In short, this book aims to help you use your Internet time more effectively by introducing you to the world of Internet search tools.

To learn more about specific aspects of the Internet, look out for my other books.

The *Net-Works Guide to the Internet* will help you learn more about the basics of the Internet. Entrepreneurs will find both *Starting and Running a Business on the Internet* and *The Net-Works Guide to Creating a Website* useful, as it deals with using the Internet to your advantage in business - saving time and increasing profits. (For more information, and to order, please see turn to the back of this book or visit our secure site at **www.net-works.co.uk** to order online.)

Chapter 1

What is the Web?

Few people in the English-speaking world haven't heard of the World Wide Web (WWW or Web for short). However, many confuse the Web and the Internet. These are two different resources and the Web constitutes a minor part of the Internet. For many users, however, the Web is the Internet.

Since its beginning as a tool developed to help research scientists disseminate documents quickly and easily, the Web has evolved to cover a wide variety of uses.

Today, you can order groceries, holidays and numerous other consumer goods online, and browse vast libraries of regularly updated information complete with photos, video and audio.

The beauty of the Web is that it allows even the most computer illiterate user to access the mind-numbing expanse of information available online - and it does this using colourful graphics, sound, animation and video!

In essence, the Web (or more accurately the Web browsers used to navigate it) hides what was previously an unwieldy collection of commands and dreary text-based menus. Instead, Web browsers display the Internet via a graphical-user-interface ("GUI", pronounced "gooey") that is simple and intuitive to use.

Once you are in the Web browser's GUI environment you can move between areas, documents and Web sites at the click of a mouse button. In essence, you can crisscross the global information maze without

> **Tip**
>
> Search Engines regularly update and modify their search functions in order to meet the increasing demands of users. It pays, then, to keep an eye on online tutorials to make sure that your knowledge is also up-to-date. Learn a little at:
>
> *www.monash.com/spidap.html*

requiring any technical understanding of how, where, why or by whom the connections are being made.

Hypertext

The power of the Web lies in the concept of hypertext.

Hypertext is the process of displaying or arranging information on a computer screen in a manner that emulates human thought processes.

In a printed book, users must read sequentially through text or manually scan pages and paragraphs (usually with the aid of an index or table of contents) in an attempt to locate information that interests them.

The human brain, however, isn't always at its most efficient when it receives information in a sequential or linear manner. For instance, you might be reading a passage of text when a word or concept catches your attention.

You could continue reading through the text, waiting patiently for the concept to be developed. But it's more likely you'll want to immediately explore that information, and will skip forward to read the connected passage, before eventually returning to where you left off.

Hypertext software allows information to be arranged and accessed in a manner similar to this. That is, hypertext documents are associative rather than linear. This is achieved by incorporating links within the text that allow users to jump to another part of the document (or another document) containing related information and then return to where they left off.

On the Web, keywords are linked to other passages or documents. Linked keywords are called hyperlinks, and are generally displayed on screen in a different colour, italicised or underlined, allowing them to be readily identified. By moving the mouse pointer to a keyword and clicking, readers are taken to the related information.

Viewing Documents on the Web

A Web browser is a software application that can interpret the links embedded in online documents and access linked documents on demand. On plain hypertext systems, all linked documents are usually on the same computer. But when this software has access

The Net-Works Guide to...

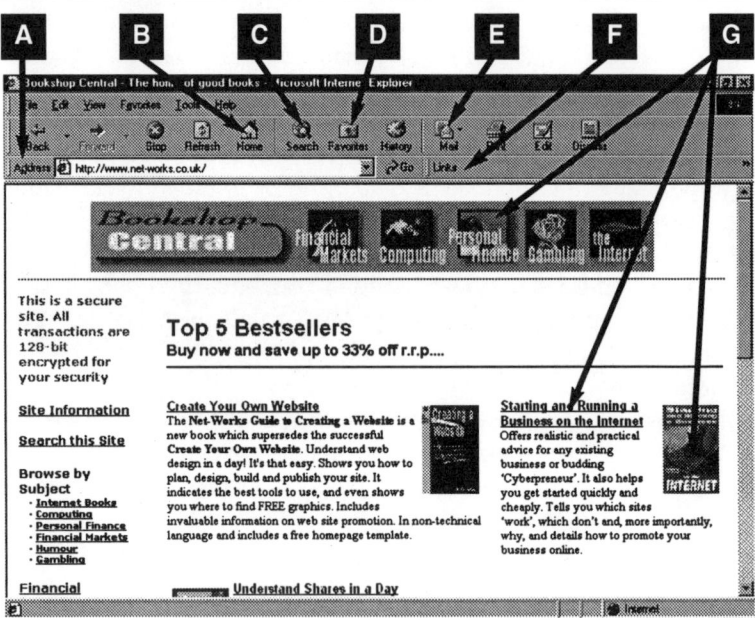

A   This is the 'URL' or address of the current Web page.

B   The 'home-page' is where you start every Internet session.

C   Click here to access a 'Search Engine' -an Internet site which can find Web pages containing key words or phrases.

D   When you discover an interesting Web site, add it to your Favourites folder so you can visit it again just by clicking this menu.

E   Click here to send electronic mail (email) across the Net.

F   Your version of Internet Explorer may have links to useful resources pre-configured when you install it.

G   Click these 'hypertext' links to visit other pages on this Web site, or other sites anywhere around the world.

12

to the connectivity of the Internet, it creates a whole new realm of information retrieval.

As mentioned earlier, Web documents can contain links that automatically connect the user to other documents anywhere on the Internet, even on the other side of the world.

You might be logged into an Australian university library via the Internet reading a document about The Endeavour. A reference to Captain James Cook is highlighted, so you click on this keyword. The link might refer to a document stored on a machine at Cambridge University in the United Kingdom. Your Web browser, in accordance with instructions contained in the link, automatically connects to the Cambridge University computer and retrieves the related document.

All of this happens seamlessly in the background. You are not required to know or understand the commands necessary to make the connection across the Atlantic, nor how to retrieve the file in question, download or view it. Those commands are pre-configured into the document, and are acted upon by the Web browser.

As you can imagine, this represents a powerful tool for accessing information, allowing even computer illiterate users to make full use of the Internet.

> **Tip**
>
> Web browsers are not limited to displaying documents. A link can contain commands instructing the browser to make ftp connections (to download software) or even connect users with Usenet groups so that they can read newsgroups.

Accessing the Web

Like most Internet resources, the Web is based on the client/server concept.

Client software (Web browsers) connect to Web servers (computers that host specific Web sites), which pass on the information or documents requested.

Today, there are literally hundreds of thousands of Web sites around the world, containing hundreds of thousands of gigabytes of information, software and graphics.

As the Web grows in popularity, more Web sites are including links to other sites, allowing users to move effortlessly across the Internet.

Tip

There are a number of excellent tutorials available online dealing with Search Engines and finding information. Have a look at this one:

www.imagescape.com/helpweb/www/seek.html

As with all Internet resources, how you use the Web depends on the software you are running to access it.

If you need help using a Web browser, such as Netscape Navigator or Internet Explorer, refer to the online help reference that comes with the software. Alternatively, a number of detailed reference guides are available at major bookshops. Failing this, you can get detailed help from the FAQ files that cover Web browsers or from Web-specific newsgroups (we discuss these in detail later in the book).

What's a URL?

URL is an acronym for Uniform Resource Locator. Every document or service on the Web has a URL, which is simply a standardised shorthand method of referring to that resource (in essence, an "address"). Web browsers interpret URLs when you instruct them to retrieve documents and perform other actions.

For example, a hypertext document called mytext.html, stored on a computer called www.example.com. in the */pub/www* directory, would have a URL of

www.example.com/pub/www/mytext.html

All the information is the same as that set out longhand in the paragraph above. However, it is recorded in a specific order: machine first, then directory, then document name. This tells the Web browser all it needs to know to connect to the specified computer and call up the document.

URLs are often used in conjunction with one of several commands, such as the **http://** command.

"http" is an acronym for hypertext transfer protocol, which is the protocol defining how information is to be sent or retrieved on the World Wide Web. By using the http:// command in conjunction with

...Searching the Internet

the URL, you instruct your Web browser to expect the document to be in Web format and act accordingly.

Specifying http:// with a URL used to be mandatory. However, modern Web browsers are quite "intelligent" and can accurately determine what type of resource you are trying to access, so you generally no longer need to use the prefix.

Specifying a URL

Most modern Web browsers respond to the "hot key" combinations <ctrl-l> and <ctrl-o> (hold down Ctrl while pressing either the letter l or o). by opening a pop-up window, into which you type the URL of the site you want to visit.

Alternatively, enter the URL directly into the Address bar (the Location bar, in Netscape Navigator), immediately beneath the toolbar. To do this, simply click your mouse in the text box, then type.

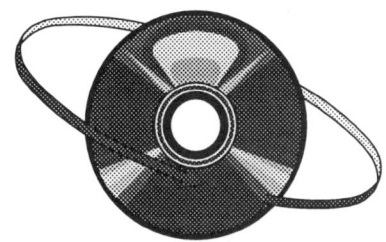

Chapter 2

The Virtual Library

Whether you are researching a project, preparing an assignment, keeping abreast of your favourite hobby, checking your team's score in the latest game, looking for holiday destinations or simply indulging in some recreational reading, you can't beat the Web - both in terms of content and accessibility.

Regardless of your topic of interest, you'll almost certainly find an information resource dedicated to it online.

The Internet offers access to magazines, books, articles, research, newspapers, newsletters and discussion papers covering the broad spectrum of human knowledge.

Formerly paper-bound government reports, court decisions, parliamentary records and national archives have been given a new lease on life - and a much larger audience - by being added to the wealth of online information.

There is now no need to wait for the next imprint of your favourite encyclopaedia to find in-depth, expert discussions of current events and discoveries. Similarly, you no longer need rely on the daily paper for coverage of community, national and international events.

During the recent Microsoft anti-trust trial in the US, interested online spectators could access up-to-the-minute court transcripts of evidence given by witnesses, as well as lawyers' statements.

Many sports events are not only beamed into the lounge rooms of millions of television watchers, but also onto the computer screens of millions of Internet users. If your favourite cricket event, for example, is not

---

Tip

Not too sure which is the best place to start your searches? Well, then, it's back to school for you!

www.connectedteacher.com/tips/searchhints.asp

...Searching the Internet

not being covered by TV or radio broadcasts, you could still follow the action via a Web site. The 70th Series - Tour of 2001, for example, will also be experienced online by millions of Internet users. Already, those interested in can satisfy their curiosity online at: ***www.334notout.com***

A New Starting Point

In the past, researchers considered the library to be the authoritative source of information. Now, however, the Internet is regarded by many as the first port-of-call in research endeavours.

Many universities and research institutes publish data and papers online. Student essays and theses, previously stowed away in archive boxes, are becoming available on the Internet. There are now entire catalogues of information, archival material and public records online to which public access was previously inconceivable. This was not because governments and libraries wanted to lock this information away, but because there was no cost-efficient way to provide decentralised access to it.

The increasing cost of traditional paper-based distribution has convinced universities, governments and businesses to invest in electronic publishing services. Researchers and Internet users alike will benefit as the barriers restricting access to information are dismantled.

Behind the hype

As any experienced Internet user will tell you, turning to the Internet for help is by no means as easy as looking in the reference section of your library for an encyclopaedia.

The Internet's wealth of information is both a blessing and a burden. Unlike resources in a library, information on the Internet is not clearly classified or categorised. You cannot, for instance, click on an icon marked Botany and have your Web browser display all Web sites containing information on plants. There is no online equivalent to the reference section, the newspaper reading area, or even the Dewey decimal system.

Almost any piece of information you might want is online, but it could be spread across tens of thousands of computers, which act as hosts for the millions of online pages. Without a central index or cross-referencing system, how can you track down a particular piece of information?

The key

The key to harnessing the information resources of the Internet, and in particular the Web, is knowing where to look.

This is not as trivial a skill as you might think. With tens of thousands of Web sites online, choosing the right starting point can make the difference between a fast, efficient search and one that is laborious. In some cases, it might also mean the difference between a successful search and a fruitless one.

In the chapters that follow, we'll examine some of the skills that make finding information online simpler and more intuitive. We'll also look at Web Search Engines and how they work to help you use these search techniques more effectively.

> **Tip**
>
> There is as yet no uniform Internet search "language". Each Search Engine varies with respect to which operators it supports and how it uses them. To determine which operators are supported, visit the Search Engine's online help pages.
>
> These are generally written in simple, easy-to-understand language with plenty of examples.

Chapter 3

The Information Chase

As children, we were taught basic information-finding skills. We all know, for instance, that libraries are an excellent resource for both fiction and non-fiction material, as are newspapers, magazines, video and film documentaries. We were taught how to use library card catalogues, how to search through footnotes and bibliographies for further references, and how to trace the evolution of a school of thought.

We were also taught that librarians, who possess an often-bewildering knowledge of the volumes that line the shelves, are there to help us. It's unlikely that many of us actually appreciate the services offered by librarians until we have to research a topic without their assistance.

The librarian's desk is, for many, the first point of call in a library.

If you are looking for a specific book or author, the librarian can usually point you to the right section, sometimes even to the right shelf.

A librarian's most useful role, however, is helping to narrow the scope of your research. You may, for instance, be looking for information on dinosaurs. If you ask for help, the librarian will first request more specific information on your search. From this, the librarian can ascertain the type of material you are looking for - for instance, whether it is archaeological or anatomical - and point you in the right direction.

> **Tip**
>
> Be careful with synonyms. If your search involves several primary search terms, do not introduce synonyms unless you include them for all the terms. Otherwise the Search Engine could respond to the inclusion of synonyms by giving them (and the related primary search term(s)) more "weight", which will affect the overall accuracy of the search.

The Net-Works Guide to...

Learning to Search

Search Engines can be seen as cyberspace "librarians".

Users submit a query, which the Search Engine uses to locate relevant Web sites and other resources. It then displays details of matched sites and resources for users to browse through and explore.

But here the similarity ends.

> **Tip**
>
> Search Engine Rule of Thumb: Every minute you spend considering and planning your search terms will probably save hours of wading through useless, unrelated links and Web sites.

While Search Engines are pivotal in helping users find their way around the Internet, they do have certain limitations.

Their massive databases of Web sites - which often contain details of hundreds of millions of Web documents - coupled with high-end computers, allow users to quickly find sites matching their queries. But speed isn't everything. Search Engines are as capable - and some would say as likely - to provide false directions with blinding speed.

There are two major causes of difficulty, each of which aggravates the other.

The first is that few people are trained in the "art" of locating information. There is more to research than simply collecting all the information available on a topic. Research requires meticulous planning and sorting.

The second problem is that many online search tools, including the majority of Search Engines, lack "intelligence". By asking a few pertinent questions a librarian can ascertain your true research goal, while the average Search Engine simply accepts the information provided and displays all matches in its database. The outcome is often search results comprised of a hotchpotch of relevant and irrelevant links.

The solution to this problem is twofold.

Firstly, Internet users need to learn research skills that will enable them to narrow their field of enquiry. Secondly, they should learn how Search Engines work - especially their advanced search options, which can be useful in filtering out irrelevant information. This book aims to instruct you in both these skills.

Search Strategies

A number of strategies can be used to make your Internet searches more fruitful and efficient. Several of these are discussed below.

Simple Searches

The easiest way to get started with Search Engines is to use simple searches. To perform a simple search, connect to your favourite Search Engine, type your query in the text box, then click on the search icon. The query doesn't have to be complex - just one or more words that describe what you are searching for (e.g. chicken soup recipe).

It's fast, simple and requires little preparation.

But it's also the type of search most likely to waste your time, since it will turn up hundreds (perhaps thousands) of irrelevant links and matches. Avoid simple searches whenever possible.

Having said that, simple searches do play a minor role in the search process. Firstly, they introduce users new to Search Engines to the searching process, and show them how fast and powerful Search Engines are (and how much information they have available).

In addition, the results of simple searches can help structure your search query to provide the best results, saving you a considerable amount of time.

For example, I wanted to locate someone online (preferably in the UK) who could value a 1906 one-penny coin I found among some old knick-knacks. For the life of me, I couldn't remember the technical name for coin collecting (which is, by the way, "numismatics", which means "of coins or coinage").

I connected to a Search Engine and used coins as my search term. There were 17,072 matches, ranging from vendors of coin purses to shareware finance programs. In the first few pages of links I

> **Tip**
>
> Seasoned Web researchers swear by the practice of starting with specific searches, then moving to more general search terms if unsuccessful. This technique, however, is really only useful if you can narrowly define your search goal at the outset.

The Net-Works Guide to...

found a reference to coin collectors, which was more specific than the search query I had used. I used this as my search term in another simple search, which returned 1,304 matches. Scrolling through the listed sites, I soon located several that interested me.

Performing one or more simple searches at the beginning of the search process can help you find additional words and phrases that you can use to construct more specific search queries. This is likely to reduce the number of irrelevant matches in your structured searches.

Plan Your Search Terms

Once you have performed a few simple searches, you will be convinced of the need to be more selective when choosing keywords.

Wherever possible, choose specific terms over general terms. For instance, the keyword yacht is preferable to boat, and chlorine will produce more useful results than chemical.

When selecting keywords, consider how other users might categorise the information you are seeking. Be aware of:

- **Spelling:**
  Some words can be correctly spelt in a number of different ways, such as grey and gray. Note the variations between British English and American English, such as center and centre, favourite and favorite, colour and color. This is particularly important given that over half the information on the Web is of US origin.

- **Synonyms:**
  Use synonyms within your search query, either by expressly including or excluding them through the use of operators (described below). For instance, where we use the words car or motor vehicle, North Americans may use automobile.

  For example, to find information on car paint, you might use a search query such as paint AND (car OR automobile OR motor vehicle).

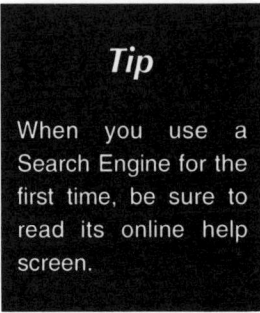

Tip

When you use a Search Engine for the first time, be sure to read its online help screen.

...Searching the Internet

This is also an example of the use of operators, which leads us to ...

Get to Know Your Operators

Almost all Search Engines support the use of operators. These are special words or symbols which, when included in a search query, give the Search Engine precise instructions on how to match Web sites to that query. This reduces the list of matches, and increases the likelihood that matched sites will be relevant. Operators are examined in more detail a little later.

Are operators infallible? Unfortunately, no.

While operators allow users to more accurately specify the information they are looking for, they don't remove all ambiguity from the search process.

Very few Search Engines are developed using the expertise of a team of librarians or other research specialists. As a result, the information they gather is often categorised in a haphazard fashion. Even if your search query is precise, imperfect indexing or cataloguing on the Search Engine's part will affect the accuracy of the search results.

Incremental Searches

Many Search Engines support incremental searches, which allow you to progressively narrow down the results of your query by refining your search terms.

> **Tip**
>
> Beware the default search format! Different Search Engines treat simple search queries differently. For example, some Search Engines use OR searches by default (that is, they match Web sites that contain any of your specified search terms) whereas others use AND searches (which only match sites if they contain all of your keywords).

For example, you might be looking for details of the benefits offered by the BUPA system over the National Health Service.

Your first step could be to connect to a Search Engine and use BUPA as your search query. The number of hits (that is, matches to your query) displayed will depend on which Search Engine you

The Net-Works Guide to...

use: for instance, at the time of writing AltaVista returned 48,370 matches, whereas Yahoo! returned only nine!

A quick look at the listings reveals that most of the sites, although covering the topic "BUPA", are irrelevant to our search, because they relate to employment, press releases, advertising campaigns and so on.

So, how can we narrow down the results on AltaVista?

The answer is simple: use BUPA, insurance and UK in the search query by typing UK +BUPA +insurance into the search box (note the space before the + sign).

Using these search terms AltaVista returns fewer than 3,600 matches. However, the search results are still quite broad as AltaVista has matched every UK service that advertises BUPA, as well as non-medical health funds that provide ancillary health benefits. But we are certainly closer to our goal than we were after our first search.

Let's try another refinement of the search, by adding the term benefits: type in UK +BUPA +insurance +benefits

This brings us closer to home. Yahoo! finds fewer matches, and AltaVista's results are more focused.

Partial Searches

If you want to perform a general search, but are unsure of the best search terms to use, try your luck with a partial search.

When performing a partial search, Search Engines look for parts of words (known as **substrings**) which match your search term.

For instance, a partial search using the term medic* will turn up matches to medical, medicine, medicate, medicare and so on. From the list of matched terms and sites you can decide which terms to follow up or which to group together when performing an incremental search.

> **Tip**
>
> When you use Boolean operators, you should enter them in ALL CAPS, with a space on either side — otherwise the Search Engine might ignore them or interpret them incorrectly.

Boolean Searches

Most Search Engines accept search queries that use Boolean operators. These include the words AND, OR,

...Searching the Internet

NOT and NEAR, as well as symbols such as quotation marks and parentheses.

Boolen operators are extremely effective filters of which sites should and should not be matched to your search query.

> **Tip**
>
> Unless you are a particularly "nononsense" searcher, try a search using a long list of related search terms before diving into advanced search techniques (discussed later). If this approach doesn't work, adopt a more focused strategy.

- **AND**

  The AND operator instructs the Search Engine to only display documents or Web sites that contain all terms joined by the AND operator.

  For example, to find only those doc-uments and Web sites containing the words mission, impossible, and movie, use: mission AND impossible AND movie. Search Engines will disregard documents containing only one or two of those terms.

  Note: Some Search Engines allow you to swap AND with +. Check the Search Engine's online help pages to find out whether it supports this function.

- **OR**

  The OR operator instructs the Search Engine to display documents or Web sites that contain at least one of the words joined by the OR operator.

  For example, to locate documents or Web pages that refer to Microsoft and/or Netscape, use: microsoft OR netscape. Using the OR operator is essentially the same as performing two searches at once (that is, performing a search for Microsoft, then a search for Netscape), but has the benefit of showing all matches.

- **NOT**

  The NOT operator instructs the Search Engine to ignore any page containing the word appearing after the NOT operator, even though it might have matched the other search terms.

  For example, to find Web sites or documents that discuss pet care, but do not relate to cats, use: pet AND care NOT cats

Note: Some Search Engines require that NOT be used in conjunction with the AND operator, so the above example would read: pet AND care AND NOT cats.

Other Search Engines allow you to swap NOT with "-" (a minus sign). For example: pet AND care -cats. Again, check the Search Engine's Help pages to find out what it requires.

- **( )**
  Parentheses are used in complex searches to group portions of Boolean queries.
  For example, to find cake recipes that use either bananas or apples, use: cake AND recipes AND (banana OR apple)

- **" "**

  Quotation marks tell a Search Engine to match only documents and Web sites that contain the search terms or phrases in the exact order in which they are entered.
  For example, to search for Web sites that discuss The Great Barrier Reef, use: "the great barrier reef"

Natural Language Processing

Search Engine engineers are busily developing technology that will allow untrained users to obtain relevant search results by typing in a plain English question (such as, "What is the average yearly rainfall in Sudan?").

This is a lot more difficult than it may sound. English is one of the most complex languages in existence. The same word can have multiple meanings, depending on the context in which it appears or, when spoken, depending on the use of inflection and non-verbal cues. Programming computers to understand not just the words used, but also the context in which they are used, is a difficult task.

While there has been progress in this field, no Search Engine can yet offer true natural language processing, although there are some respectable attempts, including AskJeeves (www.askjeeves.com).

Chapter 4

The Anatomy of a Search Engine

When the Web first appeared on the Internet, only a handful of Web sites were publicly available. Users therefore memorised address details, or kept a list of available sites.

Soon, however, the number of Web sites grew, and within a year a hundred or so dotted the electronic landscape. Memorising all these addresses was out of the question, so personal lists of sites became necessary. There was as yet no centralised list of new sites, so friends and colleagues would meet regularly (or email one another) with details of sites they had found.

Eventually, a few individuals created Web sites comprised purely of links to other sites. Yahoo!, one of the best known and highly regarded Search Engines, was created in 1994 by two university students, David Filo and Jerry Yang, to keep track of their favourite Web sites.

These first "directories" were fairly unsophisticated and rarely used any form of methodical organisation. However, as they increased in popularity, Web-based directories became better organised. Usually they were indexed alphabetically, but occasionally they were divided into broad topics.

> *Tip*
>
> The Web is in a constant state of flux and sites reorganise their materials regularly. There is no guarantee that any of the matched sites or documents will still exist when you try to visit them! If you get an error message, try shortening the URL (by removing the last directory segment or by simply entering the domain name of the site) and then navigate through this site to see if the matched document still exists on it.

These directories helped Web users find sites of interest, and this in turn stimulated interest in the Web as an information resource.

In the last few years, the number of Web sites on the Internet has skyrocketed. Today there are millions of sites online, and hundreds are added each day.

> **Tip**
>
> If you are new to Search Engines, performing a few simple searches can help you get a feel for the way in which they work.

This enormous increase has made keeping track of what is available on the Web a superhuman task.

Enter Search Engines.

Some users regard Search Engines as massive, indexed lists of Web sites and information resources, while others see them as huge databases containing information on almost every Web site available. In fact, Search Engines generally play the dual roles of Web-site directory and searchable database of sites.

Most Search Engines employ special search programs - generically referred to as spiders or Web robots - to help index and categorise this wealth of information.

These programs traverse the Internet in search of new Web sites on behalf of the Search Engine. When they find a new site, they download all the information it contains, and then carefully examine this to extract keywords and terms that can be used to index and categorise the site and its content.

These keywords are then added to the Search Engine's database, together with the site's address and a description of it.

Spiders roam the Web every day around the clock, ensuring that the Search Engines controlling them have the latest information.

The Role of Search Engines

There are essentially four types of Search Engine.

Passive Search Engines do not use spiders or similar programs. Instead, they rely on Internet users submitting details of their own or favourite Web sites. These submissions are added to the Search Engine's database.

Active Search Engines rely on spider programs to maintain and update their listings. They may also allow individuals to submit details of Web sites for inclusion - in this case, the details are

...Searching the Internet

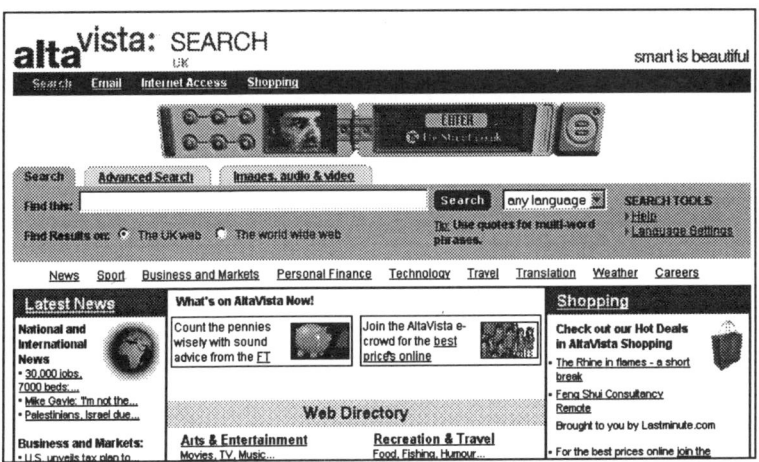

*AltaVista and Excite are active search engines.
Type your search query into the box and click on "Search"*

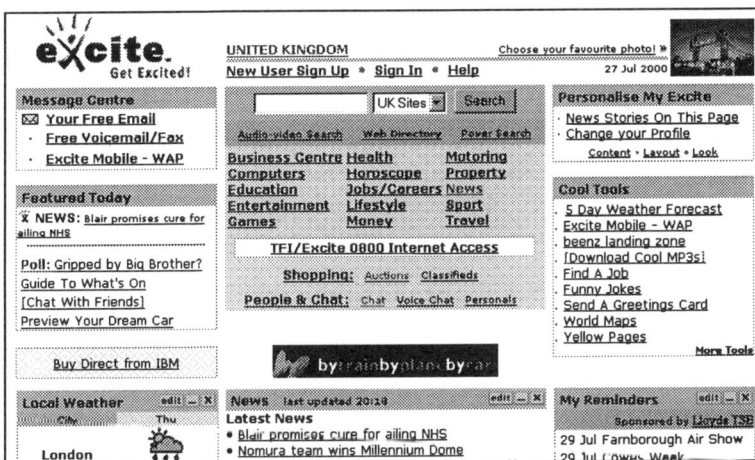

either entered directly into the Search Engine's database or passed on to a spider program for investigation.

Many Search Engines use a combination of active and passive information-gathering techniques. For example, AltaVista and Yahoo! rely on spider programs while also allowing individuals to manually submit Web site details.

Meta-Search Search Engines are not Search Engines as such, but Web sites that can be used to search several Search Engines

The Net-Works Guide to...

simultaneously. Meta-Search Search Engines (covered in Chapter 13) act primarily as user-friendly intermediaries, taking user's search queries and feeding them into several Search Engines at the same time, then sorting and presenting the combined results.

The fourth type of Search Engine has a database of Web sites compiled by human editors, who thoroughly read each new site before categorising it. These have been developed in response to complaints about the frequent inaccuracies experienced when performing general searches of massive databases.

Although these Search Engines have comparatively limited listings, they are proving popular with users. Manually compiled Search Engines include LookSmart (www.looksmart.com) and the Encyclopaedia Britannica Internet Guide (www.britannica.com).

Using Search Engines

There are generally two ways in which you can use a Search Engine: searching and browsing.

Searching

Most Search Engines provide a search or query function that can be used to locate Web sites or info-rmation of interest.

In essence, you simply type one or more keywords into a text box, and click on the search icon. The Search Engine checks its database for Web sites that match your keywords and displays these in a list.

The list of hits will generally include the name of the Web site, its address (or URL) and a brief description of its content.

To visit a specific site, click on its name - this is displayed as a hyperlink - and your Web browser will open that site.

Once a Search Engine has received your search query, it can generally search its database (which might contain tens of millions of records) and display the results in a matter of seconds. How's that for service?

> *Tip*
>
> Most Search Engines ignore commonly occurring words, such as "'a", "'and", "the" and so on, so you needn't bother including these in your search queries.

...Searching the Internet

Browsing

You may prefer to use a Search Engine to browse - casually wandering through a directory listing of sites. Browsing will take you from general headings (such as Internet, Computers, Art, Science and Sport) to specific headings (such as X-rays, Internet Chat Software, and Socceroos).

A Search Engine's main Web page usually contains a list of browseable headings that provide a categorical breakdown of the sites it has indexed. Selecting the most appropriate category for your search will lead to a page containing more specific sub-categories, which in turn will lead to sub-sub-categories or sites.

If there isn't a category specific to your topic, choose one related to it. For example, if you are looking for information on types of dinosaur, select Science as your general category, then navigate through the sub-categories to find one relevant to dinosaurs.

> **Tip**
>
> A Search Engine does not actually search the Web for sites that match your query — the search process would simply take too long. Instead, the Search Engine scans its database of previously indexed sites for matches. This enables it to provide you with a list of results in seconds, rather than days or weeks!

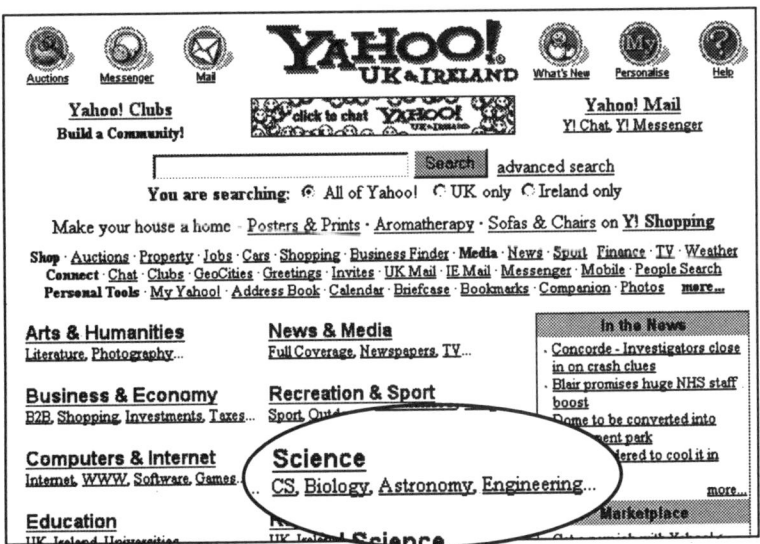

The Net-Works Guide to...

For instance, from the list of categories displayed you might select paleontology, the study of life in the geological past.

- Acoustics *(62)*
- Agriculture *(1893)* NEW!
- Alternative *(1027)* NEW!
- Amateur Science *(20)*
- Animals, Insects, and Pets@
- Anthropology and Archaeology@
- Artificial Life *(130)* NEW!
- Ask an Expert *(21)*
- Astronomy *(2516)* NEW!
- Aviation and Aeronautics *(243)*
- Bibliographies *(6)*
- Biology *(16219)* NEW!
- Booksellers@
- Chats and Forums *(44)*
- Chemistry *(1287)* NEW!
- Cognitive Science *(105)*
- Complex Systems *(23)*
- Computer Science *(1595)*
- Dictionaries *(28)*
- Earth Sciences *(2715)* NEW!
- Ecology *(691)* NEW!
- Geology and Geophysics@
- History *(92)*
- Humour@
- Hydrology@
- Information Technology *(73)*
- Institutes *(61)*
- Journals *(32)*
- Libraries *(34)*
- Life Sciences *(19)*
- Mathematics *(1862)* NEW!
- Measurements and Units *(226)* NEW!
- Medicine@
- Meteorology@
- Museums and Exhibits *(147)*
- News and Media *(144)*
- Oceanography@
- Organisations *(176)*
- Paleontology@
- People *(42)*
- Physics *(1697)* NEW!

Then, by clicking on the Prehistoric Animals sub-sub-heading, you can call up a list of sites and their descriptions.

- Extinction Theories *(18)*
- Images *(3)*
- Museums and Exhibits *(13)*
- Web Directories *(4)*

- BBC Online: Walking with Dinosaurs

- Dinosaur Hall

- Bambiraptor - newly discovered bird-like dinosaur fossil.
- Cretaceous Dinosaurs
- Dann's Dinosaur Reconstructions - mostly Australian dinosaurs information and illustrations.
- Dino Don - comprehensive information from the world-renowned dinosaur expert.
- Dino Russ's Lair - The Earthnet Info Server - provides earth science information especially in the and dinosaurs.
- Dinobase - dinosaur database with a list of dinosaurs, classification, pictures, and more.
- Dinosaur Art and Modeling - a forum for artists and modelers specialising in dinosaurs.
- Dinosaur Dreaming - research information about dinosaur cove, the Inverloch dig, polar dinosaur Cretaceous mammal.
- Dinosaur Eggs - a 1996 National Geographic Special. Watch fossil researchers as they "hatch" fo

Chapter 5

Information Retrieval Concepts

The Web's vast information resources are growing in a rapid, unstructured fashion. In fact, it can be likened to an encyclopaedia in which the contents are not alphabetically ordered, and where entries may contain references to related material from other sources.

There are several ways in which Search Engines can help you find information in this maze.

Yahoo! and Lycos, for instance, offer search functions, but place more emphasis on their hierarchical, structured categorisation of the millions of Web sites they index. These types of Search Engines act as a (incomplete) table of contents for the Web, and are preferred by users who like to browse indexes of sites.

Other Search Engines, including AltaVista, Excite and HotBot, place greater emphasis on their powerful search interfaces. These allow users to locate information and Web sites using keywords.

Although neither type of Search Engine represents a complete solution to the problem of an unstructured, poorly organised Web of information, they do at least make it easier to find what you want. Perhaps the next generation of Search Engines will close the gap.

Information Quantity or Quality

The quality of information available online is a vexing issue for Internet users.

The Internet - and the Web in particular - is the electronic equivalent of the Gutenberg press, in that it removes many of the barriers to producing and publishing information for the masses.

Almost anyone can create a Web site and publish what claims to be an authoritative exposition of a specific subject or topic. The

The Net-Works Guide to...

normal safeguards found in other forms of publishing - editors, research boards and so on - are simply not in place online.

As information consumers, we are generally trusting. Through our experience with the printed word we have come to associate printed material with authority and accuracy.

> **Tip**
>
> Sometimes using fewer search terms can be more productive. Too many search terms can lead to the Search Engine choosing the wrong term(s) as central to your search, 'skewing' the results.

Obviously, there are limits to such acceptance. For instance, if a printed pamphlet distributed by hand in the local shopping centre contradicts everything we know about a topic, we are unlikely to accept its assertions without corroborating material.

Assessing the authority of information is a skill acquired through years of experience. Few primary school children, for example, can sort truly authoritative printed material from that which contains false information.

For this reason, their studies are restricted to school libraries, where the materials available have been selected on the basis of appropriateness and content.

The research skills of high school students, however, enable them to select the most authoritative information source. When faced with material that deviates substantially from information given by known sources, they will defer to the most reputable source.

How well do these skills transfer to the Internet?

Because of the nature of the Internet, it is easy for individuals and organisations to appear authoritative while publishing what is essentially poorly researched information - or even worse, misinformation!

Levels of Authority

How, then, can you distinguish between authoritative and dubious information on the Internet?

The following sections describe the types of information available on the Internet, and how each generally ranks in terms of authoritative content.

Established Information Sources

Many well-known reference sources, such as the *Encyclopaedia Britannica*, and news and current affairs sources, such as *Time* magazine, *The Age* newspaper and *The Times*, have Web sites that provide access to their information and special reports.

Such sites can be assumed to be authoritative sources of information, in the absence of events that give rise to suspicion. For instance, in a number of cases computer vandals have broken in to Web sites and posted obnoxious material, such as nude photographs, on those sites. When visiting a site, it is almost impossible to distinguish whether information was placed there by a computer vandal or by the publisher.

If I were to connect to CNN's Web site - which would otherwise constitute an authoritative information source - and see a headline reporting that Martians had stopped by to visit the Dome, I would assume the story was a hoax or a result of computer vandals, unless it was corroborated by several other news sources.

Secondary Information Sources

This category includes research findings, official reports and publications from bodies such as universities, government committees and conferences, as well as research papers prepared by lecturers, research students and the like.

Although each individual resource might differ in value, collectively this group is reasonably authoritative. However, it is prudent to seek corroborating material.

Individual and Corporate Sites

Many individuals and companies who are experts in their fields offer access to information and materials that are second-to-none in terms of authority.

However, it is difficult to distinguish these experts from those people who use the Web as a soapbox for airing their own views, beliefs, paranoia, conspiracy theories and opinions on life and current events.

While individual sites can offer credible information, it's generally best

> *Tip*
> If you do not find a relevant link within the first 10 to 30 matches, try searching again with a modified query.

The Net-Works Guide to...

to look to other, more reliable sources before accepting the material found.

Other Research Issues

Problems with copyright and attribution also arise when using Web sites for research.

Many Internet users believe that "information wants to be free", and so don't think twice about including material from books, magazines and even other sites on their own sites. When quoting material from traditional sources, it's quite straightforward to include appropriate copyright information. But when information is published electronically, it can be difficult to verify its ownership or original source.

Similarly, attributing information found on the Web can be difficult. For instance, when quoting a passage from an essay in the Harvard Business Review, I use a standard format to attribute both the author and source. But how do I attribute a quote obtained from a Web site, a Usenet posting or personal email correspondence?

These are only some of the issues that remain to be resolved concerning the use of the Internet as a research source.

> **Tip**
>
> The order in which you specify your search terms is important to some Search Engines. Make it a habit to specify the most important terms first, regardless of which Search Engine you use.

...Searching the Internet

Chapter 6

Yahoo!

Yahoo! was one of the first Search Engines, and it remains one of the most popular.

As previously mentioned, Yahoo! began life as an online directory of favourite Web sites. Despite its transition to a billion-dollar commercial venture, it still retains much of the look, feel and structure it had in the early days.

One of Yahoo!'s prime strengths is the categorising of its content. As you can see from the screenshot below, much of the site's opening page is devoted to listing categories available for browsing. Although Yahoo! does offer a powerful search function, its strong points are organisation and structure.

http://uk.yahoo.com/

The Net-Works Guide to...

Perhaps Yahoo!'s true strength lies in the way in which it combines search features and category structure.

Yahoo! is the best port of call when you want to perform a general search, rather than look for information on a particular topic.

For example, you may be interested in motorcycles - not a specific motorcycle, such as a Ducati or Harley Davidson, but motorcycles in general. In the screenshot below, we can see that Yahoo! lists the category Recreation and Sport. Click this link and a series of sub-categories will appear, among which are Sport and Automotive.

- Amusement and Theme Parks@
- Automotive *(5589)* NEW!
- Aviation *(889)* NEW!
- Booksellers@
- Chats and Forums *(7)*
- Cooking@
- Dance@
- Employment *(7)*
- Events *(11)*
- Fitness@
- Gambling *(322)*

- Games *(16965)* NEW!
- Hobbies *(2965)* NEW!
- Home and Garden *(723)* NEW!
- Magazines *(66)*
- Motorcycles@
- Outdoors *(9251)* NEW!
- Pets@
- Sport *(39178)* NEW!
- Television@
- Toys *(831)* NEW!
- Travel *(62303)* NEW!

Following either of these sub-category headings will eventually lead to a further sub-category related to motorcycles.

- Adventure Racing *(53)*
- Archery *(160)* NEW!
- Auto Racing *(2043)* NEW!
- Badminton *(79)* NEW!
- Baseball *(4517)* NEW!
- Basketball *(3870)* NEW!
- Biathlon *(17)*
- Billiards@
- Board Sport *(17)*
- Boat Racing@
- Bobsledding *(12)*
- Boomerang *(10)*
- Bowling *(210)* NEW!
- Boxball *(1)*
- Boxing *(257)* NEW!
- Bullfighting *(27)*
- Camel Racing *(8)*

- Martial Arts *(1039)* NEW!
- Motorcycle Racing *(2)* NEW!
- Mountainboarding *(7)*
- Netball *(26)*
- Orienteering@
- Paddleball *(5)*
- Paintball *(107)* NEW!
- Pickleball *(4)*
- Polo *(39)*
- Racewalking *(16)*
- Racquetball *(36)*
- Ringette@
- Rodeo *(140)* NEW!
- Rounders *(3)*
- Rowing *(304)* NEW!
- Rugby *(679)* NEW!

...Searching the Internet

A quicker course of action would be to type motorcycle into the search box, click on the Search button, and allow Yahoo! to work its magic.

When you use Yahoo!'s search function, it retrieves and displays three kinds of information in the search results:

- All Yahoo! categories that match your search term(s) and/or contain listings that match your search term(s).
- All Web sites in its database that match your search term(s).
- Each individual Web page recorded in its database that matches your search term(s).
- It will also display - where relevant - links to recent news stories.

This breakdown provides an excellent platform for further research. Users can either drill down into Yahoo!'s categories by following the matched category headings, or jump directly to a matched site.

To continue with our earlier example, if we were to use motorcycle as our search term, Yahoo! would find a number of matches, as shown:

In fact, it found 633 categories, 3271 site matches and 27 news

- Clubs and Organisations *(31)*
- Drag Racing *(7)*
- Magazines *(9)*
- Riders *(37)* new
- Shopping and Services@
- Sidecar Racing *(17)*
- Supercross *(8)*
- Teams *(41)*
- Tracks and Speedways *(11)*
- Trials *(4)*

- Auto Cycle Union - governing body of British motorcycle sport, getting you into racing and keeping you there.
- British Speedway Promoters Association
- British Superbike Championship - news, views, and results.
- Dean Ashton Racing - British superbike race team.
- Glasgow Speedway
- History of Exeter Speedway - includes Rider Database, League tables, and World finals.
- Isle of Man TT@
- Manx Grand Prix Motor Cycle Races
- Official Lawrence Hare Web Site - a speedway rider with the Oxford Cheetahs. Keep up to date with his season.
- AMASuperbike.com - the unofficial home of AMA Superbike on the Internet. Featuring news, FAQ, columns, race results and race previews.
- American Federation of Motorcyclists (AFM) - California roadracing club. Racers, spectators, and enthusiasts are welcome.
- Army of Darkness Roadracing - endurance and sprints.
- Australian 125Gp Motorcycle Racing Page - including tuning information, bike setup, track details and bikes for sale.
- Canadian & USA Speedway Motorcycle Racing
- Canadian Superbike Championship - six-race national tour. The series consists of three professional classes superbike, open sportbike and 600 sportbike.
- Championship Cup Series (CCS)
- DirtBiking.com - with places to ride, photographs, classified advertisements, and tips.

39

stories for motorcycle. Yahoo! therefore found a total of 3931 hits (it also found a number of matching Web pages, which aren't included in the tally of matches). Yahoo! will display a list of matching categories - 20 at a time - although you can request a list of matching Web sites, Web pages or news stories.

Results of Yahoo! searches provide several different types of information sources. Using the 633 categories which relate to motorcycles, users who wish to can continue browsing, narrowing their search by locating more specific categories. Or, the 3271 specific Web sites and Web pages offer a wealth of information to users who want to jump directly to a Web site or page and begin gathering information.

Click on the Web Pages link near the top of the results page to see a list of individual Web pages that match your search term - again, these are displayed 20 at a time. In this case, Yahoo! found 196,370 matches. This is a larger number than retrieved by the other searches, as Yahoo! lists each matched Web page in its database, even if several matches are from the same Web site.

> *Tip*
>
> In addition to providing both directory and search functions, Yahoo! offers a number of excellent resources, including Yahooligans! (a children-friendly Search Engine), weather forecasts, weekly picks of the top Web sites and a chat area.

Basic Yahoo! Search Tips

- Yahoo! is case insensitive; that is, it ignores capital letters.
- By default, Yahoo! searches its database for sites and categories that contain all your keywords. This can be modified using operators.

Advanced Search Pptions

Yahoo! offers a special search page (via the options link next to the Search button) for those who wish to use its advanced search features.

These include the ability to search Yahoo!'s listings and Usenet newsgroups for information, and to search for email addresses. (note the email facility is not visible in the screenshot). Here you

...*Searching the Internet*

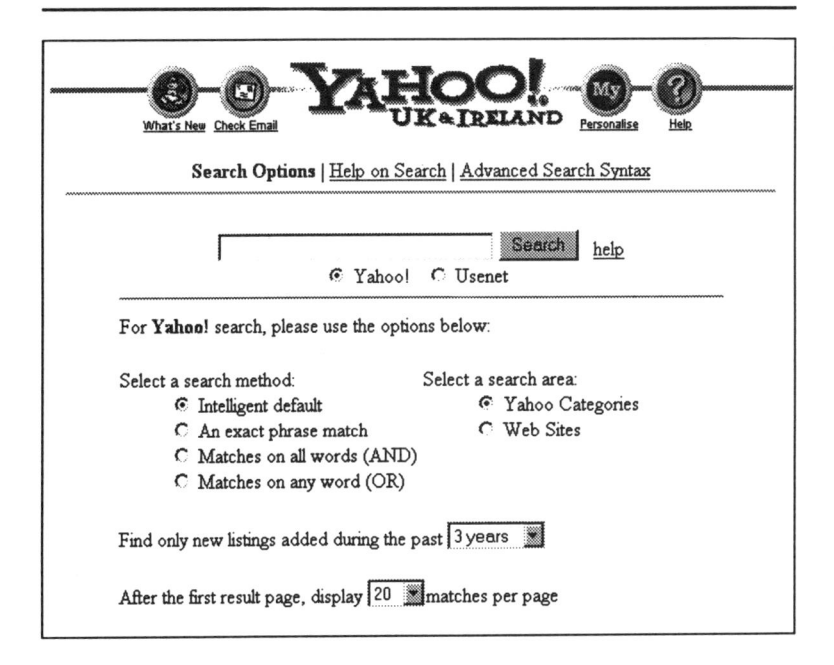

YAHOO! UK & IRELAND

What's New | Check Email | Personalise | Help

Search Options | Help on Search | Advanced Search Syntax

[Search] help
⦿ Yahoo! ○ Usenet

For **Yahoo!** search, please use the options below:

Select a search method:
⦿ Intelligent default
○ An exact phrase match
○ Matches on all words (AND)
○ Matches on any word (OR)

Select a search area:
⦿ Yahoo Categories
○ Web Sites

Find only new listings added during the past [3 years ▼]

After the first result page, display [20 ▼] matches per page

---

can also modify the number of matched categories or sites displayed on each page, and restrict your search to pages indexed within the last day - or the last three years. In addition, you can choose whether you want Yahoo! to match all of your search terms (an AND search), any of them (an OR search), or only those which are an exact match for your search term(s) or phrase in the order in which you enter them (an "exact phrase" match).

Advanced Search Syntax

- **Required Words:**
  Attaching a + to a word instructs Yahoo! to find that word in all matches. For example, if you are looking for a fiery Indian recipe, use indian +curry rather than just indian.

- **Prohibited Words:**
  Conversely, attaching a - to a word tells Yahoo! to exclude matches containing it. For instance, if you are looking for information about dinosaurs in the Jurassic era, but want to avoid links to sites which review the Spielberg movie, use the search term jurassic -park.

- **Document Titles:**
  Document titles are the names given to individual Web pages by their creators. As such, they may or may not be an accurate guide to the document's contents. To restrict Yahoo!'s searches to document titles, use the t: option. For instance, to find documents with titles containing the words lung cancer, use t:lung cancer.

- **URL Limitations:**
  To instruct Yahoo! to search only for URLs containing your search term, use the u: option. For example, to find all URLs with Microsoft in them, use u:microsoft as your search query. This can be helpful if you are looking for the domain name of a company or organisation. For instance, if you did not know the domain name used by BP, you could use this search option to locate Web sites owned by the company.

- **Phrase matching:**
  To find only exact matches to a specific phrase, place it in quotation marks. For example, to find an exact match for Ayers Rock, use "ayers rock" as your search term.

- **Wildcard Searches:**
  Yahoo! supports the use of wildcard searches, which are marked with an asterisk (*). If you insert an asterisk to the right of a partial word, such as gold*, it will find matches for gold and all words beginning with gold, such as goldilocks and goldbrick.

Full details of Yahoo!'s advanced search syntax can be found at
http://uk.search.yahoo.com/search/ukie/syntax?

For a comprehensive online tutorial on getting the best results from Yahoo!, see:
http://uk.docs.yahoo.com/info/howto/
or click the Help hyperlink in the top right-hand corner of the main Yahoo! screen.

Chapter 7

AltaVista

AltaVista made a comparatively late entry into the world of Web Search Engines. Mind you, it has certainly made up for that since it hit the streets.

AltaVista was originally designed by Louis Monier and Paul Flaherty to showcase the AlphaServer 8400 developed by Digital Equipment Corporation, which owned and maintained the site. Compaq then acquired Digital, and operated the site before selling it to CMGI Inc. in 1999.

AltaVista's developers originally planned to use the AlphaServer hardware and AltaVista search and indexing software to create a searchable index containing the entire text of every document on the Internet. AltaVista went live on 15 December 1995, boasting an index containing the full text of more than 16 million pages of online information. Within six months, this had grown to 30 million pages! The site received around 300,000 queries on its first day, and within nine months was receiving more than 19 million queries each day!

AltaVista claims to be one of the Internet's largest and fastest Search Engines - and it has some pretty impressive technology to back this claim. For example, Scooter - its custom-designed Web robot - accesses around 6 million Web pages each day, passing on information to AltaVista's indexing software, which can process more than 1Gb of text an hour. When it last published details of its database capacity, AltaVista's index contained over 200Gb of information. All this makes AltaVista an excellent research resource.

Searching with AltaVista

Originally, AltaVista only offered a search function. Now, however, it offers both extensive browsing functions, and a number of other services, such as the ability to search for images, video clips and downloadable music, plus online shopping services.

The Net-Works Guide to...

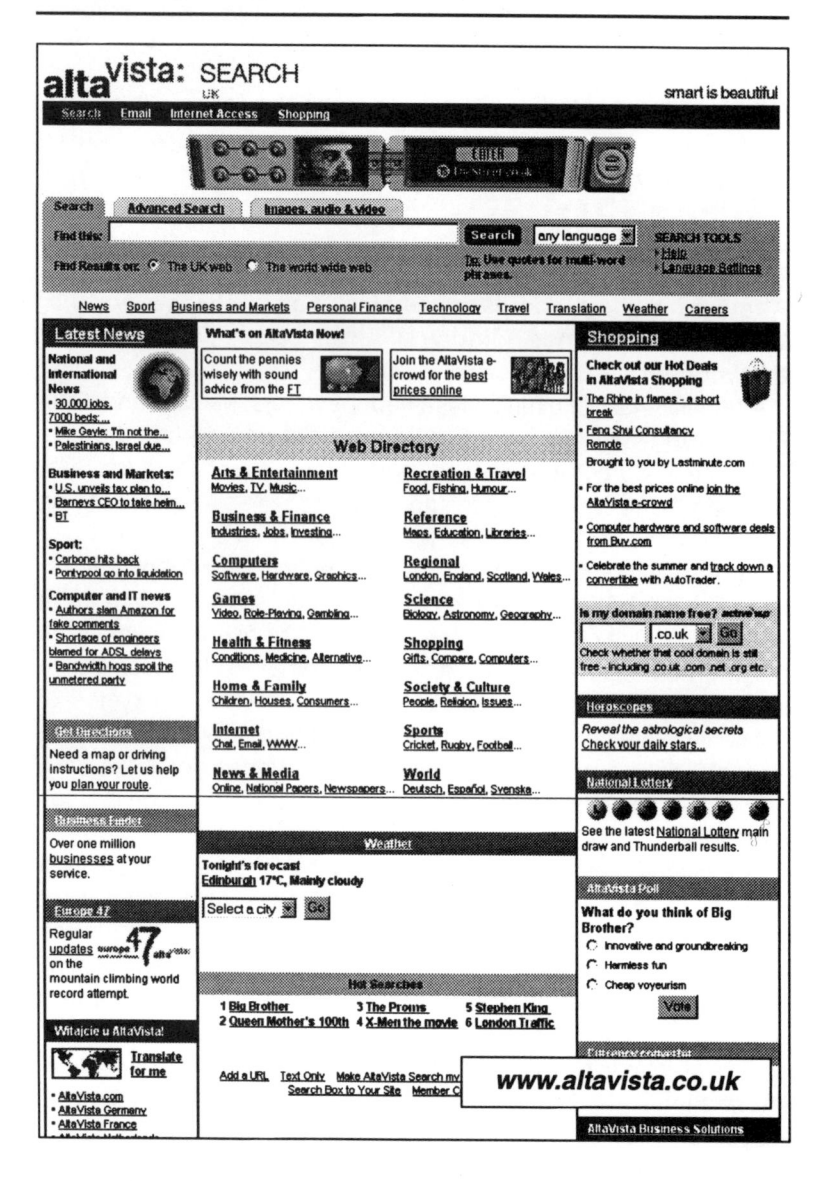

By default, AltaVista searches its database for each word used in the search query (an OR search).

As AltaVista stores the full text of every Web site it indexes, tens of thousands of matches are often retrieved, especially if your query contains general words (such as "computer", "Internet" and "car"). To reduce the number of matches, select specific keywords, or make use of AltaVista's advanced search options (discussed below).

When displaying search results, AltaVista ranks Web sites that contain the highest number of matching words first. Sites containing fewer matching words are placed lower in the list. For example, the results of a search query using the keywords British grey squirrels will list documents containing all three words before documents that only contain matches to one or two of the words.

> **Tip**
>
> AltaVista allows users to search for information in Usenet articles (rather than Web sites). To access this function, toggle the Discussion Groups option which appears immediately under the search box.

Basic Searches

By default, AltaVista performs an OR search, and list results in order of the highest number of matched words. As part of its ranking process, AltaVista also gives priority to matched pages where:

- The search term(s) or phrase(s) is found in the title of the matched document.

- The search terms or phrases are located in close proximity to one another within the text of the matched document.

- The matched document contains more than one instance of the search term(s) or phrase(s).

Advanced Searches
- **Default Operator:**
Unless special operators are included in a search query, AltaVista assumes the default operator is OR. For example, given the search query motorcycle racing, AltaVista will look for documents containing either motorcycle or racing, and display all hits. To instruct Alta-Vista to look only for documents containing all your search terns, use AND (for example, motorcycle AND racing).

The Net-Works Guide to...

- **Quotation Marks:**
  To limit AltaVista's matches to sites containing all of your search terms in the order in which they are specified, place them within quotation marks. For example, the search query "great barrier reef" will force AltaVista to only match documents containing that phrase.

- **Case Sensitivity:**
  AltaVista is very case sensitive. If you specify apple as your search term, AltaVista will return matches for apple, Apple and APPLE. However, if you use Apple or apPle, AltaVista will only match Apple and apPle respectively.

- **Required Words:**
  Attaching a + to a word instructs AltaVista to find that word in all matches. For example, to find information about pink diamonds, use diamond +pink instead of just diamond.

- **Prohibited Words:**
  Conversely, attaching a - to a word instructs AltaVista to exclude matches containing that word. For example, to find information on diamonds, while excluding information about Argyle diamonds, try diamond -argyle.

- **Wildcard Searches:**
  AltaVista supports the use of wildcard searches. If you insert a wildcard (marked with a *) to the right of a partial word (such as hydro*), it will find matches for all words begi-nning with that word (such as hydrocarbon, and hydrofoil).

  Wildcards can also be used to search for pages con-taining plurals of the search term(s), as well as to catch possible spelling variations. For example, alumi*m will catch both the English (aluminium) and North American spelling (aluminum).

- **Natural Language Searches:**
  AltaVista now supports queries submitted in standard English, such as "Where in France is the Louvre located?"

Unfortunately, like most Search Engines, this technology is still immature and needs refining.

Advanced Search Options

AltaVista offers an advanced search options page, accessed by clicking on the Advanced Web Search link on the main page (this appears on a tab directly above the Search text box).

Here users can enter search terms containing Boolean expressions, select a specific language in which to compose the search query and exclude Web sites indexed before or after a specified date.

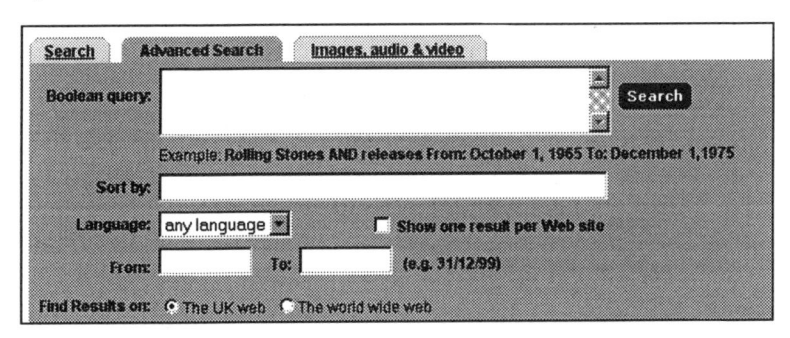

Here you can also control the way your search results are sorted. When you perform a search using the general search box on AltaVista's home page, matches are sorted by strict rules designed to ensure the most relevant matches are displayed first.

When you perform a search using the Advanced Search text box, results are shown in random order. To influence the sorting process, enter the search term(s) most important search terms in the Sort by: text box. The results will be sorted to display documents containing the specified words first.

Special Web-related Search Options

AltaVista allows users to take full advantage of its database through the use of special operators. These include:

- **anchor:**free software
  Matches Web sites that contain the specified word or phrase (in our example, free software) in the text of a hyperlink.

The Net-Works Guide to...

- **host:**net-works.co.uk
  Limits the search for matching Web pages to those contained in the nominated Web site (in this example, net-works.co.uk).

- **link:**net-works.co.uk
  Matches Web sites that contain at least one link to the specified Web site.

- **text:**Beginner
  Matches Web sites that contain the word Beginner in any part of the visible text of a page.

- **title:** "The Times"
  Matches Web pages with the phrase The Times in the title.

Language Translation

While not strictly a search resource, AltaVista's language transSlation service is certainly worth keeping in mind.

Simply enter text into the translation text box, specify the original language and the language into which you wish it to be translated, and hit Translate. Within seconds, AltaVista will display a translation. Although not all AltaVista's translations are perfect, most are useful.

At the time of writing, AltaVista offered 11 translation options, including English to French, German, Italian or Spanish, and Italian, German and Portuguese to English.

To access this feature, visit:

www.altavista.co.uk/content/translate.jsp

Tip

Librarians are very savvy when it comes to finding information, be it in books or online. So it pays to listen to what they have to say. Effective Use of Web Search Engines sounds like a dry policy paper, but it is in fact a very handy guide to using Search Engines. Read it at:

www.dpi.state.wi.us/dpi/dltcl/lbstat/search2.html

Family Filter

A growing number of Search Engines offer filtering services to ensure that Web sites with unsavoury content don't appear in search results.

AltaVista allows users to configure a filter that will block Web sites containing certain content, including pornography, violence, information about drugs and hate speech. When configuring the service you can choose which types of content should be filtered. You can even password-protect the filter, so it can't be disabled without the password.

Advanced Search Tutorial

AltaVista's comprehensive Advanced Search Tutorial outlines the search options and services offered on the site. The tutorial is packed with practical examples and is an excellent reference point for those new to online searching.

Access it at:
www.altavista.co.uk/help/search/adv_help.jsp

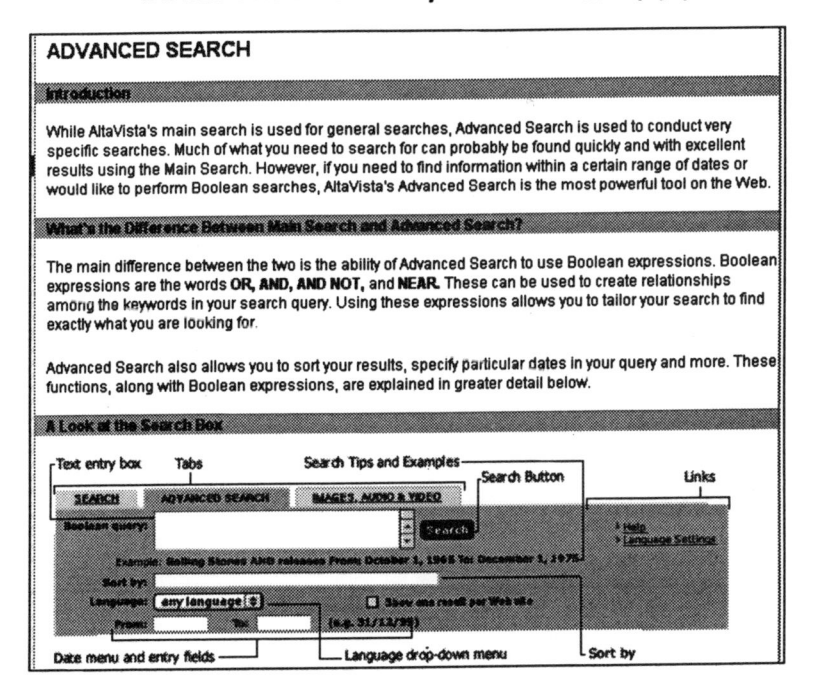

ADVANCED SEARCH

Introduction

While AltaVista's main search is used for general searches, Advanced Search is used to conduct very specific searches. Much of what you need to search for can probably be found quickly and with excellent results using the Main Search. However, if you need to find information within a certain range of dates or would like to perform Boolean searches, AltaVista's Advanced Search is the most powerful tool on the Web.

What's the Difference Between Main Search and Advanced Search?

The main difference between the two is the ability of Advanced Search to use Boolean expressions. Boolean expressions are the words **OR, AND, AND NOT,** and **NEAR.** These can be used to create relationships among the keywords in your search query. Using these expressions allows you to tailor your search to find exactly what you are looking for.

Advanced Search also allows you to sort your results, specify particular dates in your query and more. These functions, along with Boolean expressions, are explained in greater detail below.

A Look at the Search Box

The Net-Works Guide to...

Chapter 8

Excite

The Excite Search Engine offers a lot more than just search capabilities. Features inlcude the latest news headlines, weather forecasts, a customisable share tracker, sports results, technology news and more.

www.excite.co.uk

...Searching the Internet

Excite claims to have the edge over other Search Engines with its ICE (Intelligent Concept Extraction) technology. Using this technology, Excite not only scans its databases for exact matches to your search term(s), but also attempts to find pages "conceptually" linked to your query.

Tip

Want to know how Search Engines compare? You can find this information online at:

www.searchenginewatch.com

For example, if you were to search for confectionery, Excite would realise that chocolate was a related topic, and also find matches for chocolate (even if confectionery wasn't mentioned on those sites).

This aspect of Excite's search function makes it very useful for novice researchers, who might otherwise miss excellent Web resources as a result of improperly structured or narrow search criteria. Conversely, if you already know exactly what you want, it can turn up an annoying number of useless links.

Excite also extends its search capabilities beyond the Web, automatically turning up information from headline news, company information, weather reports - even stock quotes and sports scores.

Other Services

In addition to general search and information services, Excite offers a number of useful resources such as online classifieds, a people finder and an email address lookup service. It also offers a range of products for sale online - including electrical goods, music, books, flowers and gifts.

Channel Surfing

The Excite Search Engine, displays 17 browsable channels on its main Web page. Clicking on a channel calls up a detailed "channel guide", which contains links to sub-channels, a Web guide of related topics, channel-related news and events, and other novelty items.

The Net-Works Guide to...

Use the Web guide to move from general topics to specific areas and Web sites. For instance, if you select the Computers & Internet channel on the main Excite Web site, you will see many related options and links, including a Web guide featuring related sub-categories, as shown in the screenshot below.

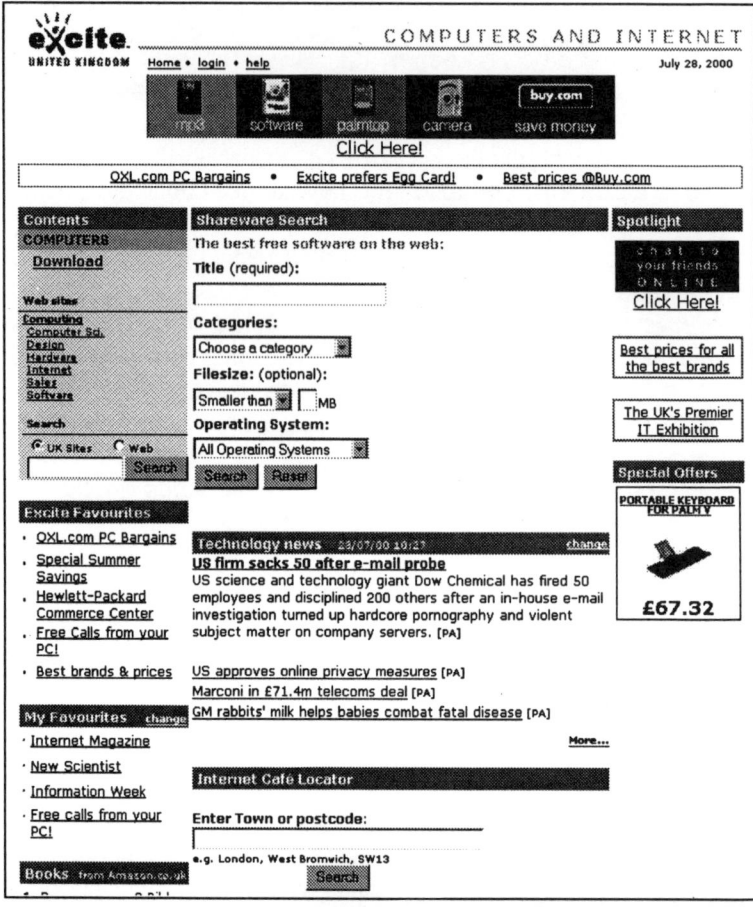

Selecting a sub-category (such as Internet) displays a list of links to related sites, as shown right:

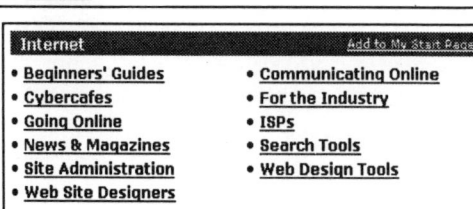

Basic Searches

To perform a simple search using Excite, type your search term(s) into the text box at the top of the home page and click on the Search button. Excite will search its database for Web sites and information sources that match both your search query and any related concepts.

You can choose to limit your search to Web sites in the UK, Europe or search the entire Web. To choose an option click on the drop down box next to the search query.

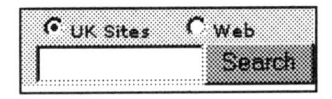

- **Default Operator:**
  The default operator is OR; that is, Excite will search for Web sites and information resources that contain any of the specified search terms. To limit Excite to a direct match of a phrase or several search terms, place them within quotation marks or use the AND operator.

- **Search Results:**
  Excite lists the matched hits ten at a time in decreasing order of relevance. Therefore, sites containing a larger number of the search terms will appear higher in the list. The list of search results displays the title, URL and a brief summary of each site. Each matched site is preceded by a percen-tage, which indicates its relevance rating.

- **Required Words:**
  Attaching a + to a word instructs Excite to find that word in all matches. For example, if you are a fan of Mel Gibson, you could use Mel +Gibson to find information about the actor.

- **Prohibited Words:**
  Conversely, attaching a - to a word instructs Excite to exclude any matches containing that word. For example, to find links to Mel Gibson but not to Mel Brooks, you could use Mel +Gibson -Brooks.

Excite Boolean Searches

If you use Boolean search operators (AND, OR, and NOT) as part of your search criteria, Excite will "switch off" its concept search capabilities and instead match only sites that meet your search criteria.

Excite Power Search

Excite's Power Search menu is used to control which sites are included in the search parameter, and is accessed from a hyperlink beside the Search button.

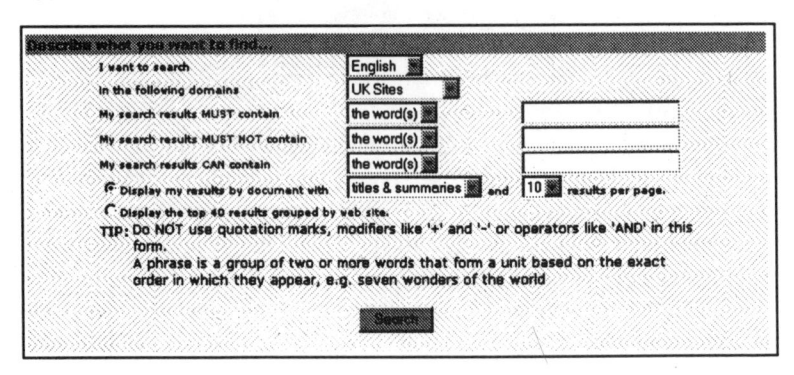

Using a series of pull-down menus, users can elect to search the entire Web (but not Usenet), or specific geographical locations, such as UK, Asia, China and Australia. Users can also specify which search terms should and should not be matched, and choose the number of results displayed per page of results.

Tip

The Online World, a free, electronic book by Odd de Presno, is a very readable guide to online resources and how to use them. There is now a Web-based version, which contains hyperlinks to sites and resources mentioned. Find it at

www.simtel.net/simtel.net/presno

Chapter 9

LookSmart

LookSmart is an Australian success story. Founded by husband and wife team Evan Thornley and Tracey Ellery in 1995, LookSmart has rapidly become one of the most prolific suppliers of directory style content for a wide range of Search Engines and online services.

LookSmart also operates an impressive Search Engine - which calls itself a "category-based Web Directory".

LookSmart does not use Web spiders or other indexing software. Instead, it employs a team of 160 professional Web researchers and editors, who explore, catalogue and summarise the content of new Web sites. Since its inception, LookSmart has developed a database of over 1 million individual URLs, indexed into more than 60,000 categories.

Although LookSmart's home page appears a little simple, it quickly becomes intuitive.

The search box at the top of the page allows visitors to perform a keyword search of LookSmart's catalogue of Web sites.

Below the search box are 13 broad categories, including Entertainment, Business, Travel, Computing and Library.

The site also features news headlines, financial information, encyclopaedia, dictionary and atlas search functions and online shopping services.

LookSmart Centres feature content and services related to popular topics, including business, finance, jobs, automotive and technology. For instance, the automotive centre features news and magazine articles from the car industry, financial and loan tools (such as calculators), prices of new and used cars plus links to automotive-related categories within the main LookSmart Web site.

By default, LookSmart limits itself to UK-only Web sites. To display sites from around the world, click on the tab labelled The World above the list of sub-categories. Select a top-level category from the home page to view a list of sub-categories.

Choose a sub-category, and a list of sub-sub-categories is displayed. Select one of these, and either a further list of categories is shown, or links to specific sites, or a combination of both, depending on the number of categories in that topic.

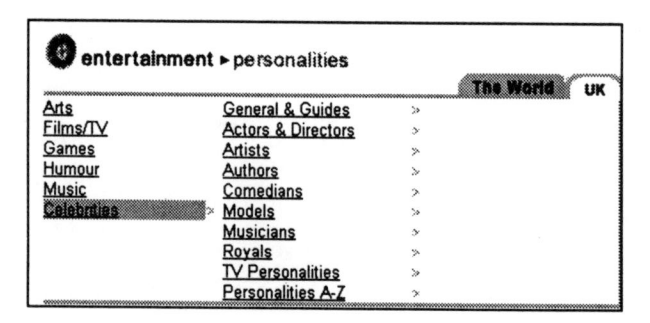

entertainment ▶ personalities		
		The World UK
Arts	General & Guides	≫
Films/TV	Actors & Directors	≫
Games	Artists	≫
Humour	Authors	≫
Music	Comedians	≫
Celebrities ≫	Models	≫
	Musicians	≫
	Royals	≫
	TV Personalities	≫
	Personalities A-Z	≫

For example, if I select the Entertainment top-level directory, I am shown the sub-categories Arts, Celebrities, Games, Humour, Movies/TV and Music.

Selecting Celebrities displays a list of sub-sub-categories, including Authors, Models, Artists and Musicians.

Selecting Models takes me to a list of related Web sites.

Searching with LookSmart

As mentioned earlier, LookSmart's search function can be used to quickly locate matching sites in its database. While this database is dwarfed by those belonging to other Search Engines, the quality of its listings is exceptional. To boost the number of search results, LookSmart also automatically scours the AltaVista Search Engine and include matches from its extensive database.

LookSmart supports advanced search operators (such as AND and OR), but they are not required.

Search results will include up to three levels of information, where relevant.

First, the results will display matching LookSmart categories. Clicking on a matching category will take you to a list of Web sites in that category.

The results will also show a list of matching Web sites in the LookSmart database. In addition, the category in which the site is listed within the LookSmart directory and a summary of the site will be displayed.

Finally, the search results will show matches received from the AltaVista Search Engine.

Chapter 10

Lycos

The name Lycos is derived from Lycosidae, a family of wolf spiders noted for actively pursuing prey, rather than relying on the passive device of a web. This family of spiders, which is closely related to the Tarantula, is also well regarded for its speed over the ground. Presumably, Lycos' creators hoped their choice of name would appeal to Internet users who want fast, pro-active search solutions.

For many years, Lycos sported a spider-like logo, although it has now abandoned this in favour of a less ferocious-looking motif.

Search with Lycos

Lycos caters for both keyword searches and browsing.

The main Web site features a search box, 14 broad directory headings, links to 12 Topics, free software, online auctions, message boards, news headlines and various online shopping services.

Search Basics

Lycos' extensive database contains the full text of every Web site and document it has indexed. However, redundant words, such as "the", "and" and "a" have been purged. Therefore, it will ignore these words if you use them as part of your search query.

Enter your search terms in the search box, then click on Go Get It!.

Tip

Lycos offers extensive, user-friendly help for those new to searching. Simply click on the Help link next to the search box, or go to:

http://www.lycos.co.uk/help/search.html

...Searching the Internet

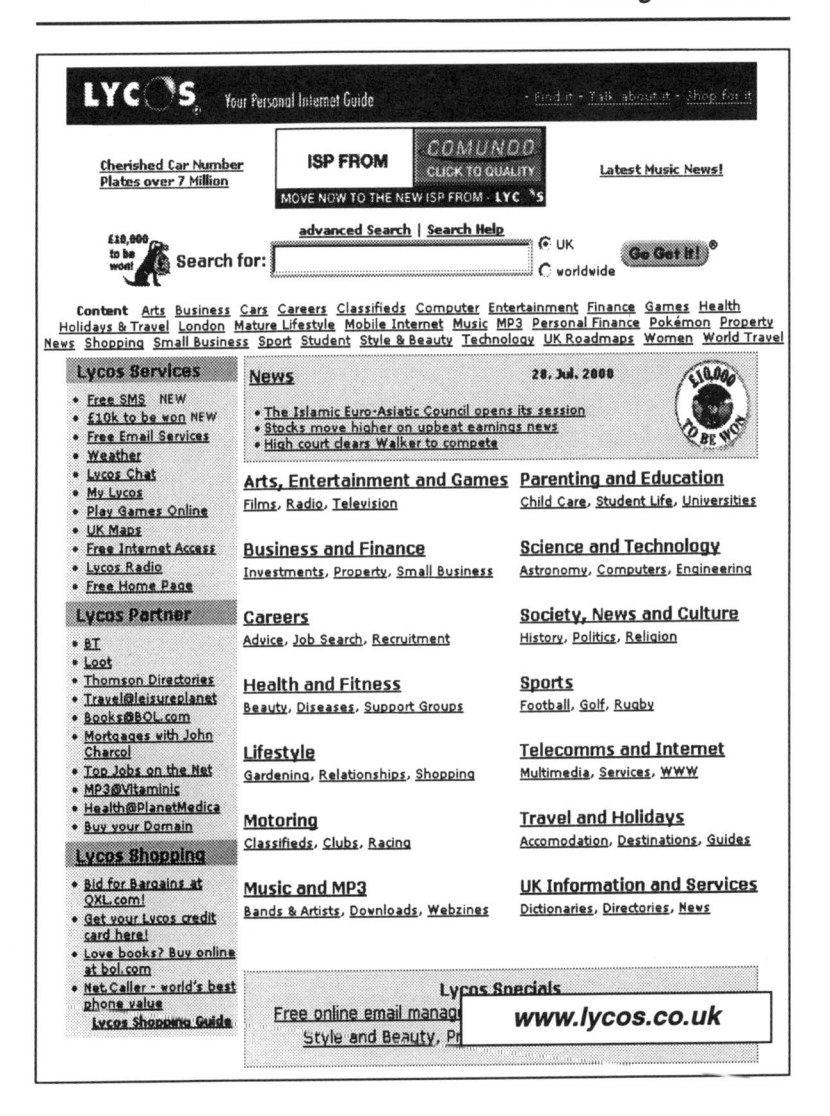

[Screenshot of Lycos UK homepage at www.lycos.co.uk showing search box, category listings including Content, Arts, Business, Cars, Careers, Classifieds, Computer, Entertainment, Finance, Games, Health, Holidays & Travel, London, Mature Lifestyle, Mobile Internet, Music, MP3, Personal Finance, Pokémon, Property, News, Shopping, Small Business, Sport, Student, Style & Beauty, Technology, UK Roadmaps, Women, World Travel; Lycos Services, Lycos Partner, and Lycos Shopping sidebar sections; and news headlines dated 28 Jul 2000.]

Lycos will display a list of search results, divided into four main categories: matching Web sites selected by the Lycos editors on the basis of quality and relevance, matching Web sites, matching news or media reports, and matching Lycos shopping categories (that is, matching products or services).

The results will also include a list of suggested additional search terms to help narrow general searches.

Advanced Search Options
Lycos supports a number of search operators, including:

- **Prohibited Words :**
  To exclude words from Lycos searches, use the - sign. For example: season -salt

- **Partial Words:**
  To match partial words, use the & symbol. For example, pig& would find pig, piggery and pigeon. This can be useful when you are searching for someone by name, but are not certain of the correct spelling.

- **Specific Phrase:**
  To match a specific phrase, enclose the words in quotation marks.

Browsing Lycos' Directory
Lycos features an easily navigable directory of sites, listed under categories such as Computers and Internet, Science & Technology, Health and Reference. Several major sub-directory headings are also displayed beneath the corresponding directory heading.

> **Tip**
> For more information about how Search Engines work, visit The Spider's Apprentice:
> www.monash.com/spidap.html

Selecting Reference, for example, displays the Lycos Reference Directory, which features numerous sub-directories and links to reference resources around the globe. Many of Lycos' resources are hand-selected by a team of expert editors and researchers, so you can be sure they are worth exploring.

Lycos Custom Searches
Lycos' Advanced Search page is accessed by clicking on the Advanced Search hyperlink beneath the search box.

...Searching the Internet

From the default Advanced Search page you can opt to perform a range of searches in addition to a Web search, including a search for multimedia files, maps, downloads, recipes and news. You can also specify whether Lycos should use an AND or an OR search as the default, or whether it should search for a specific phrase.

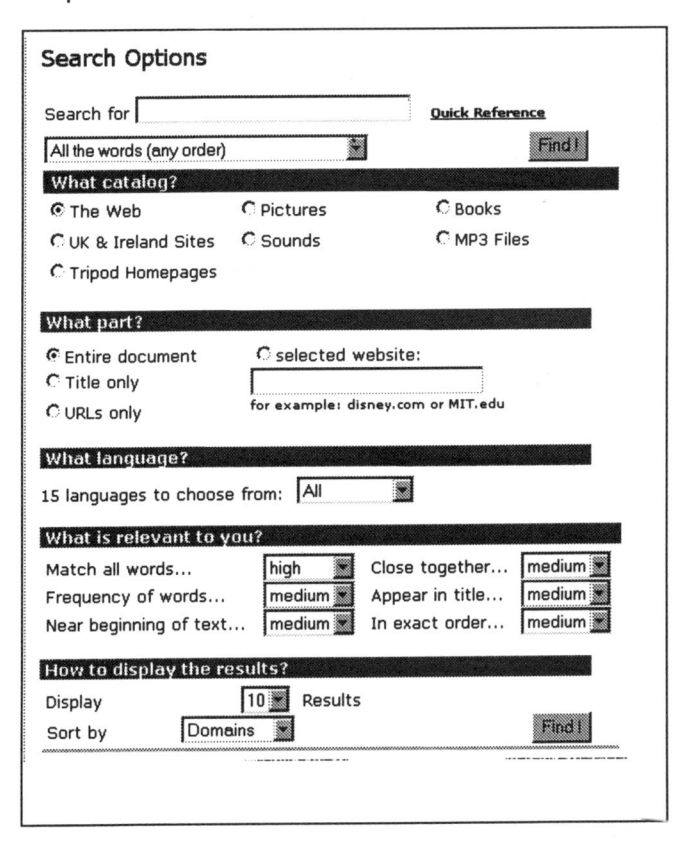

- **Search For:**
Selects whether matched words should appear within 25 words of each other.

- **Display:**
Modifies the number of hits that Lycos displays per page of results.

61

- **Results:**
    Specifies how Lycos should rank the importance of various search factors, such as word frequency.

There are three other configurable Advanced Search options:

- Click on the Page Field link to choose to refine your search by matching your search terms to specific titles, URLs or domain names.

- Click on the Language link to limit your results to Web documents written in a specific language.

- Click on Link Referrals to search from Web sites or Web pages that link to specific Web sites and pages.

...Searching the Internet

Chapter 11

GO.com

GO.com, the search engine that used to be Infoseek, has adopted the simple, "utilitarian" approach favoured by Yahoo!. It lacks the overly glossy, graphic-laden look and feel of other major Search Engines, and concentrates on being powerful and wide-ranging. Founded in January 1994 as Infoseek to provide Internet users with access to useful, quality information, today it continues to fulfil this aim under the GO.com banner.

GO Network is a collection of impressive and well-known Internet sites, including the US ABC News Web site (www.abcnews.com), the Disney Web site (www.disney.com) and the ESPN sports Web site (www.espn.com). Membership to this group of sites allows Infoseek to offer users additional access to premium content and a wide range of services.

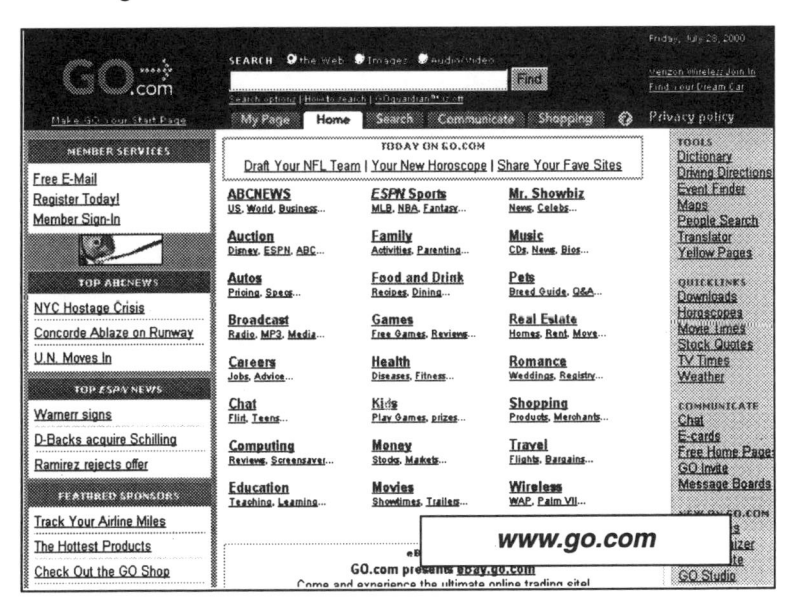

www.go.com

The Net-Works Guide to...

Seeking Information with GO.com

GO.com's main Web site offers multiple layers of information in addition to the standard search box and directory listing. You'll also find the latest news headlines, US stock quotes and links to services such as horoscopes, movie reviews, "e-cards" (multimedia greeting cards that are sent electronically) and more.

The Web Directory, which contains a detailed list of GO Guides or subject categories. Select the Communicate tab to access the InfoSeek Community, where you'll find links to topical online chat rooms and message boards, or select Shopping for links to some of the best buys online.

GO.com has a multicultural flavour, offering versions of the site in languages including French, German, Italian and Japanese.

Basic searches

GO.com's home page offers browseable 21 directory headings and a search box. The directory structure is similar to that of other popular Search Engines.

Click on a directory heading to move to a page containing a detailed list of sub-headings. From there you can jump to pages containing more specific headings and site listings. Each listed site is summarised, so you can tell if it is appropriate to your needs.

...*Searching the Internet*

To initiate a basic search, type a query into the search box, then click the Find button. By selecting a radio button above the search box you can choose to search the Web, or to search for images, audio files or video clips.

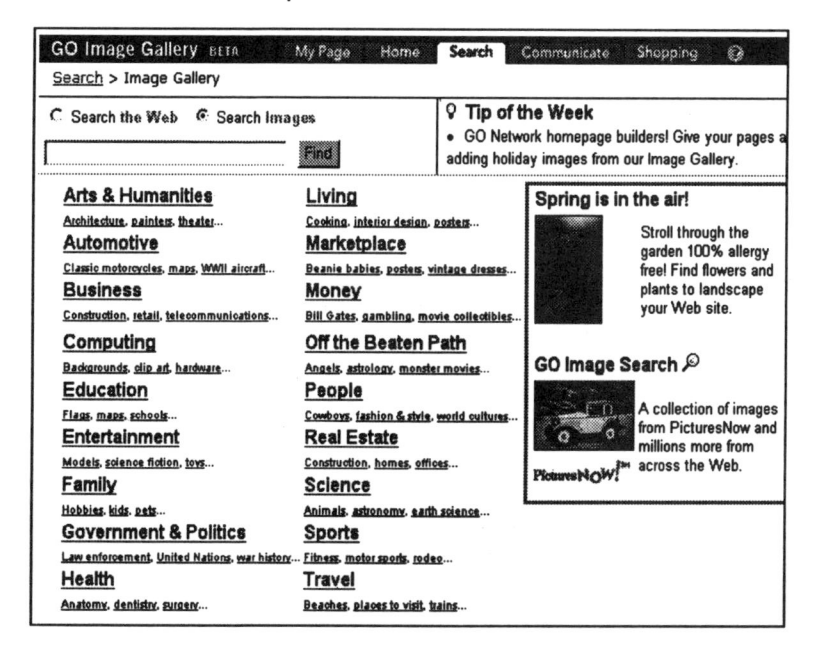

Search Options

To refine your search, click the Search options link beneath the search box. This will display an advanced search interface.

GO.com supports standard search operators, including AND, OR and NOT. It also supports the use of + and - symbols to expressly include or exclude words. Note that the search process is case sensitive, so 'go' is considered to be different to 'Go'.

From the advanced search interface you can choose to search documents, titles or URLs, or look for a name, word or phrase.

In addition, you can select a tab to perform customised searches, as discussed below:

- **Web:**
  Here users can specify search parameters, and choose to search the entire Web, a specific country or just the InfoSeek Web directory. In addition, the format of search results can be controlled.

- **Usenet:**
  Perform customised searches of Usenet newsgroups.

- **Companies:**
  Accesses online databases containing information on thousands of (primarily US) companies.

- **News:**
  Search a collection of "news wires" from original news sources, such as Reuters, Business and PR Newswire. Even if the wires have not been featured in mainstream publications you can use them to track news issues.

- **Reference:**
  The Reference screen is divided into sub-categories, and allows users to search for maps and driving directions, look up words in a dictionary and thesaurus, or scan domain names and classifieds.

Advanced, Web-specific Search Options

GO.com supports a number of operators that restrict searches to certain portions of Web sites or documents:

- **link:net-works.co.uk**
  Matches Web sites that contain at least one link to the specified domain name or Web site. Here the site specified is maximedia.com.au This is useful for finding reviews of your favourite Web sites and resources.

- **site:microsoft.com**
  Limits the search to information on a specific Web site.

- **URL:net-works**

...Searching the Internet

Matches Web sites or pages which contain the specified word in their URL.

- **title:net-works**
  Locates Web sites or pages with the specified word in their title.

GOguardian

Recognising the concerns of parents over the possibility of children encountering adult material online, GO.com offers a search filter to automatically block adult or selected material from search results.

Parents who register with the free GOguardian service can also select a password. Once enabled, GO.com will filter adult content from search results. GOguardian protection can be turned on or off at any time by clicking on the GOguardian link beneath the search box and supplying the password

---

Search with GOguardian

Search with GOguardian ™
Now with optional Password Protection!

There are some things on the Internet that you probably don't want your kids to see. GO Network is concerned about this too, so we developed the GOguardian.

When GOguardian is turned on, you can search the Web without seeing any inappropriate adult content. GOguardian filters out objectionable material, so you can feel more comfortable allowing young people to explore the Web on the GO Network. (In addition, all searches in the Kids and Family Centers automatically use GOguardian whether it is turned on or not.)

GOguardian now includes *optional password support. The primary user of a computer can set up a password for GOguardian for each web browser on that computer. Then, anyone using those web browsers on that computer will be protected from inappropriate adult content while using GO Network's search features. Before any user can search with GOguardian turned off, he or she will need to enter the password first.

Choose one:
○ GOguardian on
◉ GOguardian off

Enter your password: *optional

Need to set up a password?
[OK] [Cancel]

67

Chapter 12

A New Generation

Today's Search Engines, which offer information, news, sports, weather, horoscopes, auctions, classifieds, maps, telephone directories, free email and shopping services, are becoming too unwieldy to be of much use.

New users are easily confused by the number of options that confront them on the home page, and experienced users are disgusted by the increasing amount of screen space dedicated to advertising.

A new breed of streamlined search services is starting to appear.

Led by Search Engines such as Google (www.google.com), these services are returning to their more modest origins by offering only a powerful search interface.

Google

Google has taken a new approach to Web searches. Instead of matching Web documents based on the number of times your search term(s) appear in them, Google uses PageRank technology to determine a document's popularity.

PageRank assumes that the more Web sites or Web pages that link to a particular Web document, the more likely it is that the document contains relevant, authoritative information.

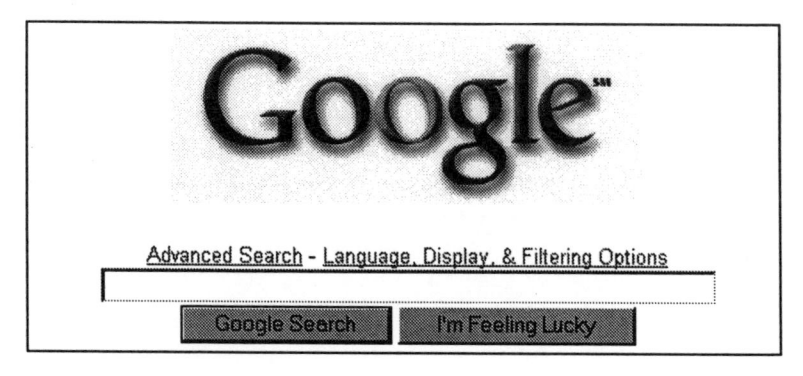

In essence, each link to that document is treated as a "vote" for it. A document with more votes is treated as more "important" than one with fewer votes.

Google then analyses the "importance" of the Web pages or sites containing links to the document. If these are important, their votes are given added weight. If a Web page that is frequently linked to by other Web pages in turn contains links to more pages, those pages are given even greater weight.

This process allows Google to exclude irrelevant matches and better structure the list of displayed matches.

And, thanks to the fact that the Google Search Engine contains little "fat" - due to the absence of advertising and other extraneous materials - it completes the searching and matching process very quickly indeed!

Caching

Google has extra hard disk capacity that allows it to "cache" (that is, store copies of) many Web pages. This allows it to display a matched Web page even if the Web Server it is located on is temporarily unavailable or the Web page has been recently moved or deleted.

Performing a Search

To perform a search with Google, enter your search term(s) in the search box and click on the Google Search button. Google automatically searches for documents containing all your search terms.

Google doesn't support OR searches, as it always tries to match documents containing all your search terms. It also doesn't support wildcard searches (that is, partial words entered in with an asterisk e.g. medic*). Finally, Google isn't case sensitive, so Apple, aPpLe and apple are treated equally.

Google does support searches for specific phrases, providing they are enclosed within quotation marks (for example, "great barrier reef"). To streamline results, Google ignores commonly occurring words, numbers and prefixes (which it calls stop words) such as and, http:// and .com

To specifically include stop words, prefix them with a plus sign (+). For example, to perform a search for Windows 98, use Windows +98.

Rapid Searching

If you are in a real hurry, click on I'm Feeling Lucky instead of Google Search. Google will perform your search in the same way, then automatically connect you to the first matched document.

Search Results

Google provides rapid search results. For instance, a search for Off Piste Skiing resulted in 57 relevant matches and took only 0.07 seconds!

Google displays its search results 10 at a time. At the top of the search results you'll see statistics about the search process, including the number of matches found and how long the process took.

Below this are categories Google considers to be relevant. These can be browsed in the same way as you would browse categories or directories in other Search Engines.

Next, Google displays the first 10 matched documents. The search results include the title of the matched Web page or document, a brief description of the site, its size and URL.

If Google finds multiple Web pages on the same Web site, it will display only the two most relevant matches. The second match will be slightly indented from the list of results to indicate it is from the same Web site as the preceding match.

To view a matched page, simply click on its name. If it won't appear for some reason, click on the Show matches (Cache) link to load it from Google's cache (when available).

Finally, if you find a particularly good match, click on the Similar pages link to display a list of similar matches.

Raging Search

Raging Search (www.ragingsearch.com) is a relatively new offering from AltaVista. While it uses the same technology and database as the main AltaVista Search Engine, it lacks the extraneous advertising and content of its parent site.

To search, simply type your search term(s) in the search box and click on the Search button. The search options are identical to those used by AltaVista.

To access Raging Search's customisation service, click on the Customize link beside the Search button. From here you can configure the Family Filter, select the language you wish to search in, specify the number of search results displayed, automatically translate matched pages and more.

Oingo

Oingo (www.oingo.com) is another streamlined Search Engine, in the same vein as Google and Raging Search, but with an interesting twist.

Oingo bills itself as a "meaning based" Search Engine. This means it employs technology that allows its search software to understand both the specific meaning of your search terms and the context in which you use them.

For example, performing a search for "Darwin" could turn up references to Charles Darwin, to the capital city of the Northern Territory, to several other cities around the world or to a little-known operating system developed by Apple Computer Inc.

When Oingo performs a search, it returns a standard page of matching results. To streamline these results, you can specify the meaning of each of your search terms. Where more than one meaning is possible, a drop-down menu lists those available.

Select the meaning most relevant to your search from the list of word definitions displayed by Oingo, then perform a search again - and revel in the relevant matches that appear!

The Net-Works Guide to...

Oingo currently offers little support for advanced search options. It performs an OR search by default (that is, matching any of your search terms). It does not support AND searches - use the + sign to specify words that must be matched.

Ask Jeeves

Although Ask Jeeves (www.ask.co.uk) is not essentially a new-generation Search Engine (it offers a range of extra services as well as searching), it warrants a mention in this chapter due to the novel way it helps users locate information of interest.

Ask Jeeves supports questions asked in plain English, such as What is the distance between Mars and Venus?

It first interprets your question using its natural language processing technology to determine both the meaning of the words and of the grammar used. It then scans its database, which contains several million questions and their answers (7 million at the time of writing), to find the most relevant answer. If Ask Jeeves doesn't have a specific answer to your question, or if it's not sure how to interpret your question, it will display a list of similar questions for which it has located answers. You then choose the one closest to your initial question.

As an added service, Ask Jeeves submits your question to several other Search Engines and summarises their results in the results page.

...Searching the Internet

Chapter 13

Meta-Search Engines

Meta-Search Engines are a Web-search enthusiasts' friend. In fact, they can cut your research time in half. How?
A Meta-Search Engine is not a true Search Engine. It does not have its own database of sites, nor does it employ a search spider. Instead, Meta-Search Engines exist to help users search multiple Search Engines at the same time. In essence, a Meta-Search Engine submits your search query to several different Search Engines, then collates and displays the results it receives.

Meta-Search Engines were developed because users were growing tired of searching one Search Engine only to find few or no matches, then receiving tens of thousands of matches from another. In essence, they provide users with the best of both worlds.

byteSearch

byteSearch (www.bytesearch.com) is a quick and powerful Meta-Search Search Engine.

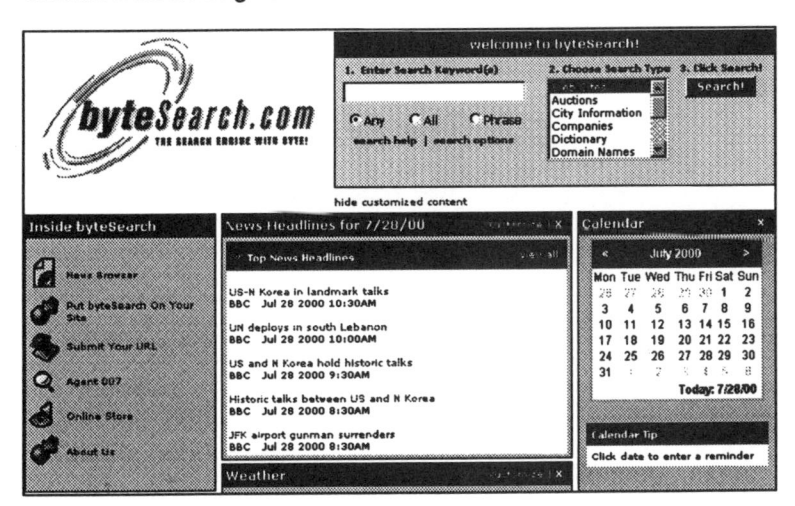

73

byteSearch is a quick and powerful Meta-Search Engine that will submit your search query to the major Search Engines and compile an aggregated list of search results (up to 150 matches).

In addition to searching the Web, byteSearch can search news reports, look for multimedia files, search for company information, check weather information and scan Usenet newsgroup postings.

byteSearch's results include details of which Search Engine made the match, and a hyperlink that allows you to repeat the search using only that Search Engine.

For the curious, byteSearch offers the "Agent 007" service, which displays a list of the last 20 search queries submitted (a word of warning: it's likely the queries in this list will include sex-related terms).

Metaeureka

MetaEureka (www.metaeureka.com) takes "streamlined searching" seriously. It promises a no-nonsense search experience, with no graphics whatsoever.

Just enter your search term(s) in the search box and click the Search button. Within seconds, MetaEureka will display a page of aggregated search results, 35 matches at a time.

MetaEureka's Search options are brief and to the point. You can opt to include either 10 or 20 matches per Search Engine in the results, and choose whether or not you want a description of each matched site displayed.

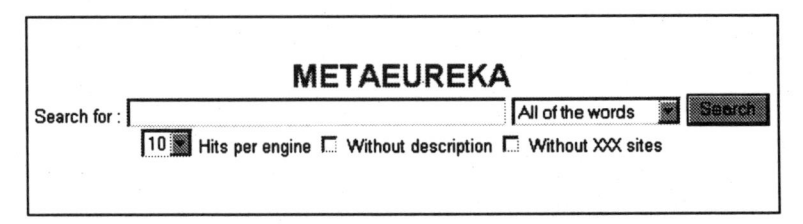

METAEUREKA

Search for : [_____] [All of the words ▼] [Search]

[10 ▼] Hits per engine ☐ Without description ☐ Without XXX sites

---

MetaCrawler

MetaCrawler (www.metacrawler.com) was conceived as a Master's degree project by Erik Selberg and his advisor, Oren Etzioni, at the University of Washington. Now part of the Go2Net network of content sites, it supports a number of major Search Engines including AltaVista, Excite, InfoSeek, WebCrawler and Lycos.

...Searching the Internet

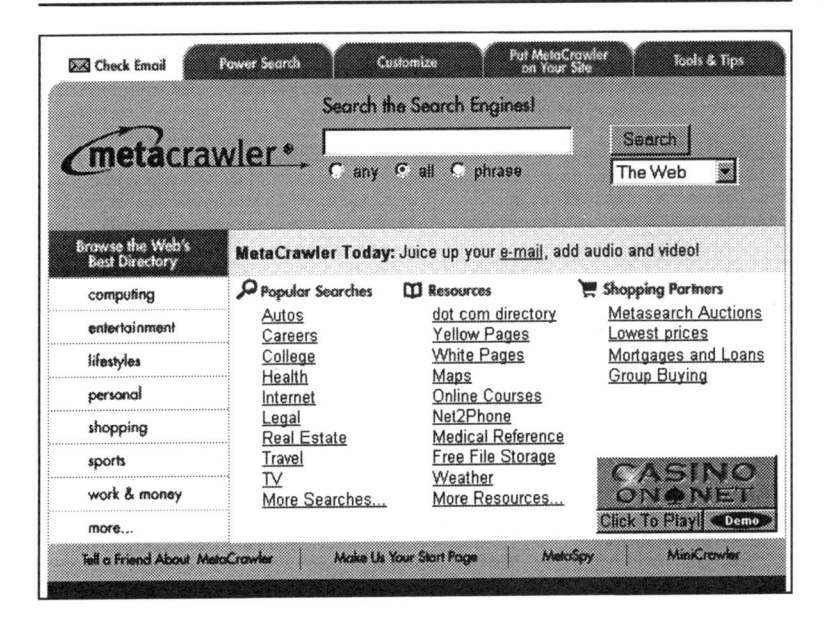

Composing searches is simple. Type your search term(s) in the search box, then select the "any", "all" or "phrase" search option. From the drop-down menu below the Search button choose to search the Web, Usenet newsgroups, look for images or multimedia. Once you have completed your search query, click the Search button.

MetaCrawler submits your query to each Search Engine in the format most appropriate for that Engine. More importantly, it reorders all hits in terms of relevancy, removes duplicate matches, and displays the results as a single list.

All this makes it an indispensable tool for Internet researchers.

MetaCrawler now also offers a Power Search interface, accessed by clicking on the Power Search tab. From here you can specify which Search Engines to search and order the manner in which MetaCrawler outputs its results.

The BigHub

The BigHub (www.thebighub.com), formerly Internet Sleuth, is something of an oddity. Although its claim to work with over 1,500 search databases may sound incredible, it's not stretching the truth!

The Net-Works Guide to...

Searching with The BigHub

The main Web site provides users with a search box from which they can poll eight major Search Engines (including AltaVista, Excite, InfoSeek, Lycos, and Yahoo!).

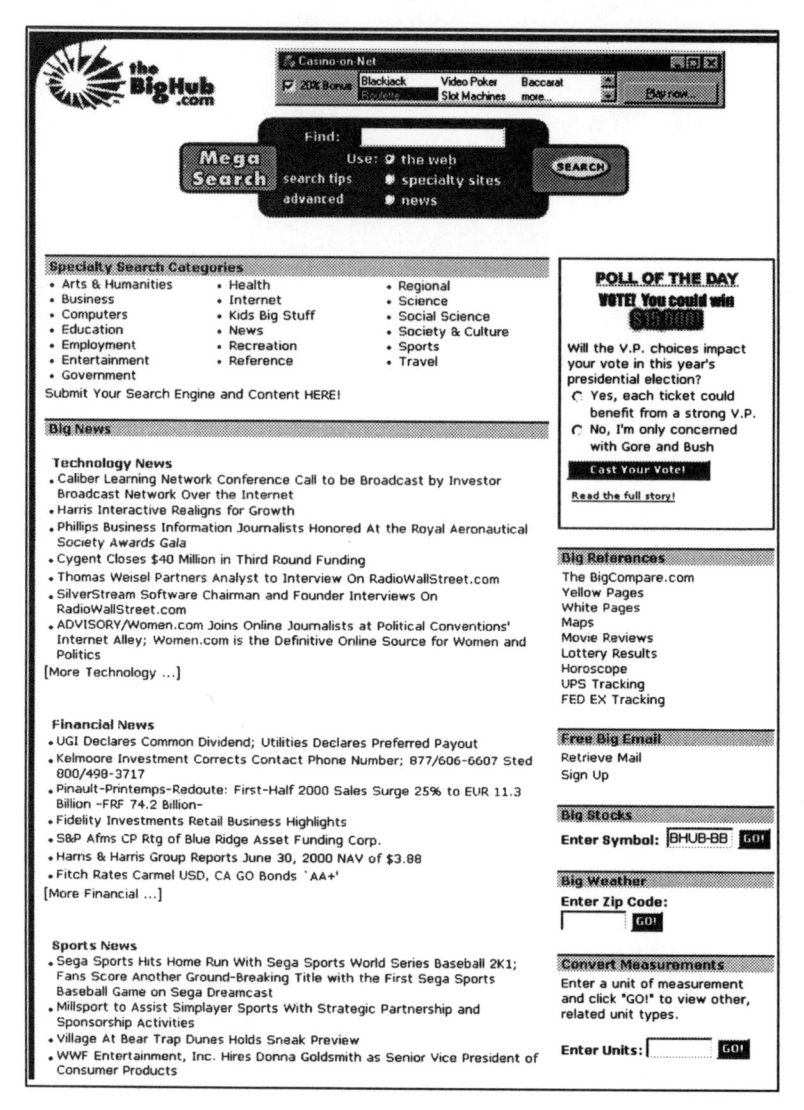

Type your search term into the search box, then use the checkbox beside each Search Engine to indicate whether it should be included in your search. Select how long you are prepared to wait for the results from each Search Engine (up to 20 seconds), then click on the Search button.

Results from the first Search Engine or Web resource polled will be displayed on a single page. If more than one page of matches is retrieved, these will be accessible via links.

Browsing with The BigHub

The BigHub offers a comprehensive, browseable list of search categories. Click on a category to view a customised search page, from which you can perform a search using one or more of the listed search services.

InFind

InFind (www.infind.com) works with the six largest Search Engines - WebCrawler, Yahoo!, Lycos, AltaVista, InfoSeek, and Excite, polling each of these in parallel, thereby reducing search delays.

To enhance the search process, InFind merges the results reported by each Search Engine, removes duplicate matches and displays results according to relevance. (Relevance, it should be added, is determined by InFind - a fact that can lead to some interesting and questionable ordering.)

In order to maximise the potential of each query, InFind polls some Search Engines several times. For instance, whereas Yahoo! allows you to request 100 matches per page, InfoSeek will only display 10 results at a time. Therefore, InFind will poll InfoSeek several times, in order to extract a larger number of matches.

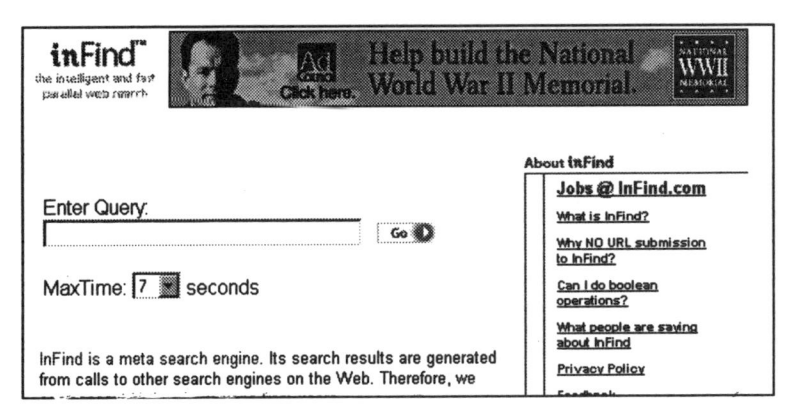

ProFusion

ProFusion supports several Search Engines, including Excite, InfoSeek, Yahoo! and AltaVista. It operates in much the same fashion as other Meta-Search Engines, by combining results and removing duplicate matches. ProFusion supports both Web and Usenet searches. In addition, ProFusion offers two important services, discussed below.

Automatic Pick Best 3

By default, ProFusion analyses your search query, then selects which three of the Search Engines it supports will give the best results. It uses these for your search.

Alternatively, users can opt to have ProFusion use all supported Search Engines, the fastest three Search Engines, or manually specify which Search Engines they want to use. You can select the search type by clicking on the relevant radio button.

Personalised searches

ProFusion allows users to register with its free personalised search service, MyProFilter, which records details of your most frequent searches. Users can later return to the site and ask MyProFilter to automatically perform these registered searches.

This is a time-effective way to monitor Web sites to see if they have new or updated information on your research topic.

Other Meta-Search Engines

Meta-Search Engines are becoming quite popular, and there are now quite a few available. You may want to experiment with those listed below:

Mamma	www.mamma.com
WebTaxi	www.webtaxi.com
All4One	www.all4one.com
C4	www.c4.com
SavvySearch	www.savvysearch.com
Search Spaniel	www.searchspaniel.com
SurfWax	www.surfwax.com
DogPile	www.dogpile.com
MetaGopher	www.metagopher.com

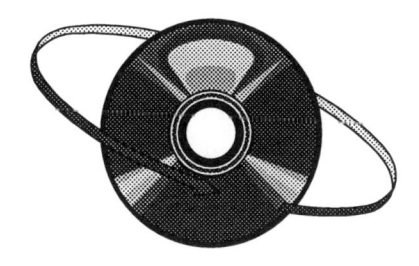

The Net-Works Guide to...

Chapter 14

Finding Someone Online

One of the most perplexing aspects of the Internet is that there is no easy way to ascertain someone's email address. The main reason for this is that there is no central authority charged with issuing email addresses. As such, no one is in a position to collate them.

The best advice I can give to people who want to obtain someone's email address is to simply call that person and ask! Hardly the pinnacle of technological progress, but that's the way it is.

Email directories

Having said that, there are a number of online email directories that attempt to provide a White Pages solution for email addresses. In essence, these are huge databases of email addresses collected over the years. They have a simple search interface, into which you type the name of the person whose email address you are seeking.

The fundamental flaw of these directories is that there is no obligation for anyone to actually register with them. Therefore, the directories have to find other means of collecting email addresses.

The standard trick is to filter Usenet postings, which usually contain both the name and email address of the person posting the message. The problem with this is that not everyone uses Usenet, so there are many people whose email address won't be listed.

When using an email database remember that these programs can't easily distinguish between indiv-

> **Tip**
>
> In a bid to become the biggest and the best, some email directories neglect their housekeeping. In researching this chapter, I came across a number of my former email accounts - some of which I have not used since my university days almost a decade ago!

iduals with the same name. Don't be surprised, then, if more than a dozen different email addresses match one name. And it may be that none of these belongs to the person you are trying to locate! But, if you are in a pinch and need to find someone's email address (and can't otherwise contact them), email directories and email Search Engines are worth a shot.

> *Tip*
>
> Although many people regard online 'people finder' databases as a convenient, free service, others find them intrusive - and who can blame them? It is now possible for US Internet users to search White Pages listings, and retrieve not only an individual's telephone number and street address, but also view a street map with the person's house marked.

Bigfoot

Bigfoot (www.bigfoot.com) has been around for some time, and over the years has amassed quite a collection of email addresses.

In addition to providing email address search facilities, Bigfoot allows users to search the White and Yellow Pages (only US-based, unfortunately), request email reminders of important dates and even apply for a free email address.

To search Bigfoot's database, type the name you are searching for in the search box, toggle the email addresses check box, and click on the Go button. Bigfoot will then display a list of matches.

The Net-Works Guide to...

Meta Email Search Agent (MESA)

MESA (http://mesa.rrzn.uni-hannover.de) is, in essence, a people-finding Meta-Search Engine. MESA will submit your query to a number of different email directories and databases, and collate the results.

Enter the *Name* of the person:

First Name: Mark
Last Name: Neely

markn@piperstudiosinc.com
- *(Yahoo People Search)*

3) **Neely, Mark P**

neely_mp@darwin.ntu.edu.au
- *(IAF)*

4) **Neely, Mark,**

mnaaa@aol.com
- *(Bigfoot)*
man13@aol.com
- *(Bigfoot)*
102232.2276@compuserve.com
- *(Bigfoot)*
ACCESSNT@ozemail.com.au
- *(Bigfoot)*
CCESSNT@ozemail.com.au
- *(Bigfoot)*
mpn@infolution.com.au
- *(Bigfoot)*
MHamiltonN@aol.com

Remember, however, that by polling several databases at once, you not only increase the chance of finding a match, but also increase the chance that the matches you find won't be for the person you want. For instance, a search for Mark Neely turned up the email addresses shown in the shot below. Determining which address is the right one is a matter of educated guesswork and following up leads.

Yahoo! People Search

Yahoo! People Search (http://people.yahoo.com) is one of the more sophisticated online email directory services.

In addition to a simple search page, it offers an advanced email search service that can dramatically reduce the number of mismatches.

Among the advanced features Yahoo! People Search offers is the ability to limit searches by geographic region, domain name or company name.

For instance, if you know Uncle Bob has an email account with example.com, or uses a company email account provided by Smith & Co., you can limit your search accordingly, thereby increasing the accuracy of results.

Yahoo! People Search also uses "smart" name matching, with the result that, for example, searches for "Robert Smith" will also match "Bob Smith".

Welcome, Guest User   Create My Listing - Sig

Advanced Email Search

Fill out as much or as little information as you want. All fields are optional. Enhance your search by choosing organization name and type.

First Name		Organization Name
Last Name		
City/Town		Organization Type
State/Province		○ Company
Country		○ University/College
Domain		○ High School
Old Email Address		○ Military
		○ Other
		⦿ All Organizations

☐ SmartNames™ (Bob = Robert)

[Search] [Reset]

Internet Address Finder

The Internet Address Finder Web site (www.iaf.net) boasted 6,720,664 listings at the time of writing - quite a few email addresses, indeed.

In addition to searching by first or last name, users can restrict searches to specific domain names or organisations. However, this option is really only useful if you know where the person whose email address you are searching for works, or the name of his or her ISP. As people are likely to change ISPs more often than jobs (although you never know!), the organisational field will probably be of more use to searchers, although this assumes the individual has accesses email at work.

To send an email message to a matched email addresses, simply click on it.

Chapter 15

Other Research Options

If you read through a collection of Internet magazines and books, you will be hard-pressed to find information on Internet resources other than the World Wide Web. The Web, it seems, is the be-all and end-all of Internet resources. After all, who can ignore the exciting, multimedia world of graphics, sound, images and text it offers?

However, by restricting your research to the Web alone, you may miss out on other important and potentially timesaving information resources.

This chapter looks at three further avenues for information gathering: FAQs, email discussion groups and Usenet. It also takes a brief look at the world of online libraries.

Just the FAQs

The term "FAQ" stands for Frequently Asked Questions. An FAQ file, then, is a document that contains a list of frequently asked questions on a given topic, as well as answers to those questions. There are hundreds of FAQ files available on the Internet, covering a broad selection of topics.

FAQ files were created both to help Internet users, and to minimise the time wasted answering questions posed by "newbies" (that is, inexperienced Internet users).

There are tens of thousands of newsgroups and email discussion groups available on the Internet, some of which deal with very specialised topics. Many regular participants have been following these discussion forums since their inception. Over the

> **Tip**
>
> Even if you cannot find the answer to your question in a FAQ file, it will probably contain links to Web sites with related information. These pointers can help you to track down other useful resources.

The Net-Works Guide to...

years, they have canvassed dozens of topics, joined in heated debates, chas-tised members for inaccurate comments, and even taken time off for personal chitchat and gossip.

It soon became obvious to these veterans that each new generation of forum participants came in search of the same answers, and the forum was wasting time by answering the same questions time and again.

To solve this problem, participants volunteered to collectively author FAQ files, which all newcomers are invited (or occasionally instructed) to read before posting questions to the group. Newcomers usually find that their questions have been answered in the FAQ file and, having been brought up to speed, can join in the current discussions.

FAQ files therefore represent an excellent source of information.

Copies of FAQ files written in Usenet newsgroups are posted to the newsgroups on a regular basis (usually monthly, but occasionally weekly). You can also find a collection of FAQ files in the news.answers newsgroup, which is the central point of distribution for many FAQs.

Even though FAQ files are regularly posted to Usenet newsgroups, there is no guarantee they will be available on the day you look for them. If you can't find the FAQ file, try one of the FAQ archives on the Web:

> **Tip**
>
> Ask for help! It is unlikely that your problem is unique. Someone, somewhere, has probably succeeded after hours of trial and error in finding the information you seek. If your initial attempts turn up nothing, or are less satisfying than you had hoped, post a request for help in relevant newsgroups and email discussion lists.

Mad Hippy FAQ Archive www.madhippy.com/faqs/
FAQ Central www.faq-central.net
The FAQts www.thefaqts.com
Internet FAQ Archive www.faqs.org

Most of these FAQ archives use basic "text string" matching search techniques. That is, they search each available FAQ to see

> **Tip**
>
> You can also subscribe to mailing lists via a Web page, such as Mailing List Web Gateway *(www.netspace.org/cgi-bin/lwgate)*. Simply search the list of available email discussion groups to find one of interest, then follow the onscreen prompts to subscribe.

if it contains any of the keywords you have specified. If it does, it is considered a match.

To avoid multiple irrelevant matches, avoid common terms (such as FAQ and Usenet) and don't even bother with terms that are guaranteed to appear in every FAQ (such as Internet).

Email Discussion Groups

Email discussion groups are an excellent resource, both for a quick answer to a particular question and in-depth understanding of a topic that interests you.

Most email discussion groups are two-way lists. That is, a copy of each message you submit to the discussion group is sent to every other subscriber (and there may be thousands), and a copy of each message submitted by other subscribers is sent to you.

Some email discussion groups have a fairly low "traffic" rate, and only generate a handful of messages each week. Others can generate 10, 20, even 50 messages a day!

Special email automation software is used to co-ordinate the discussion group. This software adds new members to the group, and removes those who ask to leave.

Joining such groups usually involves sending an email message to a special email address, such as:

listserv@example.com.uk

with a command in the body of your email similar to:

subscribe <name of list>Your Name

New email discussion groups are usually advertised (or "announced") in short postings to related Usenet newsgroups, outlining how interested users can subscribe or who to contact for further information. However, it is unusual for existing groups to be advertised (unless they are actively recruiting new members). In this case, try one of the Web sites below. These contain a searchable list of discussion groups, allowing you to look for email lists that cover your area of interest. They generally also provide instructions on how to join the discussion groups, or who to contact for more information. In fact, most now handily offer a Web-based interface for subscribing and unsubscribing to mailing lists.

eGroups	www.egroups.com
List-of-Lists	catalog.com/vivian/interest-group-search.html
Liszt	www.liszt.com
Publicly Accessible Mailing Lists	
	paml.alastra.com
Tile.Net Lists	tile.net/lists/
L-Soft List Search	www.lsoft.com/lists/list_q.html
Topica	www.topica.com

For a detailed list of mailing lists divided into ready categories, visit:

www.yahoo.com/Computers_and_Internet/Internet/Mailing_Lists/

If you are successful in subscribing to (that is, joining) the discussion group, you will receive an email message from the discussion group automation software confirming your subscription. Read this message carefully (and print or save a copy for safekeeping). It will contain administrative information, such as who to email in the event of problems, how to unsubscribe, and general rules of behaviour. More importantly, you will usually be pointed to the group's FAQ.

Before you ask a question in an email discussion group, download and read any FAQs available in the forum. Most Internet users are happy to lend a hand, but many will be annoyed if they are faced with a user who hasn't made any attempt to research the problem first.

To find out more about how email discussion groups work, visit:

The International Federation of Library Associations and Institutions Internet Mailing Lists Guides and Resources
www.ifla.org/I/training/listserv/lists.htm

Usenet

Usenet newsgroups (often also referred to as "Internet newsgroups" or just "Internet news") are an excellent source of information - both in terms of FAQs and the willingness of Usenet participants to answer questions.

To participate in Usenet discussions, you generally need a newsreader program. If you use either Internet Explorer or Netscape Navigator you have all the software you need, as these browsers both feature built-in newsreading capabilities.

If you don't have a newsreader program, you will need to download and install one. There are a number available (usually free or shareware) for both Mac and Windows-based PCs.

For a fairly exhaustive list of newsreader software and for Usenet resources, visit **www.newsreaders.com**. Alternatively, ask your Internet Service Provider or computer administrator for a newsreader program.

Usenet newsgroups work in a similar manner to email discussion lists, with one vital exception. When you create and post a message (known as an article) to a Usenet newsgroup, it is uploaded to a Usenet server.

Instead of being automatically distributed to everyone who reads that newsgroup, the article is stored online and can be down-loaded by participants. Therefore, each Usenet newsgroup acts like a noticeboard, and articles sent to newsgroups are displayed in a public forum that anyone with newsreader software can read.

Given that Usenet newsgroups have a potential audience of millions, you can be confident that someone will help you with your query, or at least point you in the right direction.

There are two ways in which another Internet user may respond to you.

The participant can note your email address (which is usually automatically included in your article when you post it) and respond to you privately by email.

Alternatively, that participant may compose an article in response, and post that to the newsgroup, so that both your question and the answer are available to all newsgroup participants.

To find out more about Usenet, visit these sites:

New User Questions -
www.geocities.com/ResearchTriangle/8211/
Zen & The Art of the Internet
www.cs.indiana.edu/docproject/zen/zen-1.0_6.html

Deja vu?
Not everyone has the time to follow newsgroups in the hope of eventually finding the information they want. Often you need answers now - not tomorrow or next week.

There is an easier way to search Usenet newsgroups for articles of interest, and it is called Deja - www.deja.com/usenet

Deja offers a powerful search interface aimed at Usenet newsgroup articles. It works in a similar manner to Search Engines, but instead of indexing Web sites, it indexes newsgroups and the articles that have been posted to them.

Although most Search Engines allow you to search Usenet as well as the Web, none is especially designed to perform Usenet searches. This means that Deja often has the advantage.

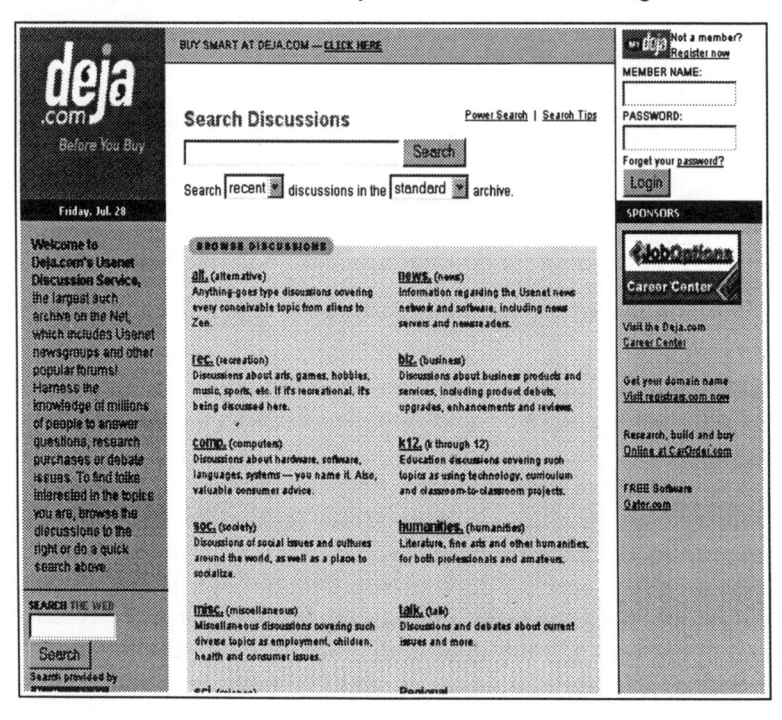

...Searching the Internet

Deja offers both a Quick Search and a Power Search interface. When using Quick Search, users type their search terms (with or without operators) in the search box and click on the Search button.

Deja's Power Search interface (accessed by clicking on the Power Search link next to the search box on the main page) gives users more control over the search process, including whether to perform AND or OR matching, whether to search through current or archived news articles, and how matches and summaries should be displayed.

I performed a search using cloning sheep as my search terms. Admittedly, I was not entirely sure what Deja would turn up.

Deja found 55 matches, in newsgroups ranging from sci.bio.technology (a newsgroup discussing biotechnology) to alt.religion.scientol (a newsgroup for discussing Scientology).

Date	Subject	Forum	Author
07/21/2000	Re: Cloning and Souls	alt.religion.mormon	Ldzion
07/27/2000	Re: TEST!!! DON'T READ	alt.toys.gi-joe	Jeffrey Griffin
07/27/2000	Re: TEST!!! DON'T READ	alt.toys.gi-joe	THOR
07/26/2000	Re: [VERIFIED] Secret Govern	alt.paranet.ufo	Sir Arthur Whol
07/21/2000	Re: Cloning and Souls	alt.religion.mormon	Mrs. Murphy
07/20/2000	Re: Cloning and Souls	alt.religion.mormon	C&C
07/20/2000	Re: Cloning and Souls	alt.religion.mormon	Mrs. Murphy
07/18/2000	Cloning and Souls	alt.religion.mormon	Mrs. Murphy
07/18/2000	Re: Cloning and Souls	alt.religion.mormon	geoff matthews
07/21/2000	Re: Non-Traditional Families	alt.genealogy	W F Sill
07/18/2000	Re: Cloning and Souls	alt.religion.mormon	Tyler
07/13/2000	Re: Sheep (was Re: The troub	soc.culture.thai	David Shorter
07/06/2000	Sheep (was Re: The trouble w	soc.culture.thai	Roscoe
07/10/2000	Re: "HARRY POTTER" BOOK RECA	misc.writing	Kurt Ullman
07/09/2000	Re: male nurses	sci.med.nursing	Kurt Ullman
07/09/2000	Re: male nurses	sci.med.nursing	Kurt Ullman
07/09/2000	Re: male nurses	sci.med.nursing	Kurt Ullman

Deja's list of matched articles includes details of when the article was posted, which newsgroup it was posted to, and who posted it.

To read an article, simply click on the subject title. Deja will display the full text of the article, then allow you to view related newsgroup articles (click on the Threads hyperlink) or post a response to the article you are reading (using the Post Reply icon).

The Net-Works Guide to...

Deja is a very useful tool, allowing users to quickly scan thousands of newsgroups for articles of interest to them. A similar service, with a slightly different interface, is available at the remarQ Web site (www.remarq.com).

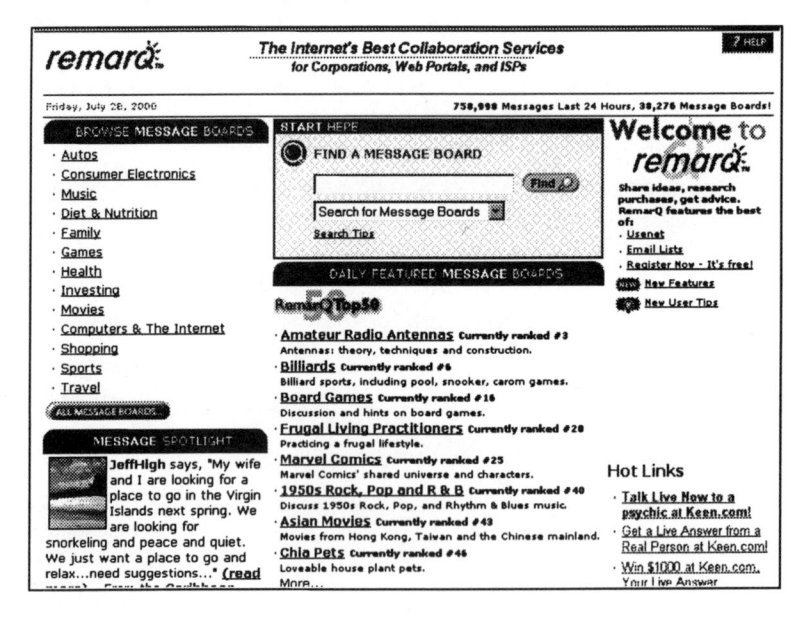

Virtual Libraries

You might try all the resources discussed in this book and still not find the information you want.

There could be several reasons for this. For instance, you might not be proficient at using search tools. Alternatively, you might not be couching your search queries in the right terms, or, very possibly, the information you want might not be available online.

Whatever the reason, don't despair. You have one last port of call - a virtual library.

Virtual libraries, as their name suggests, are Web sites designed using the same principles as traditional libraries. As such, they tend to be carefully organised, extensively cross-referenced, and contain materials chosen on the basis of information quality.

Virtual libraries generally fit in one of two categories: general reference or specific reference libraries.

General reference libraries attempt to tie together the major resources available on the Internet, then categorise and catalogue them.

On the other hand, specific reference libraries seek to provide an exhaustive index of all online resources relating to a single, defined topic.

Which virtual library you use depends on what you are looking for, and how you prefer to search.

The Internet Public Library

The Internet Public Library - www.ipl.org - is a true gem.

While its Web site might not be the most graphically oriented or intuitive site around, it is expertly indexed into bite-sized chunks.

The categories available at the Internet Public Library site mimic a real library's layout. For instance, there is a reference section, an area containing magazines and serials, and an online text area (containing over 12,000 items at the time of writing). There are also plenty of links to other electronic library sites and related resources.

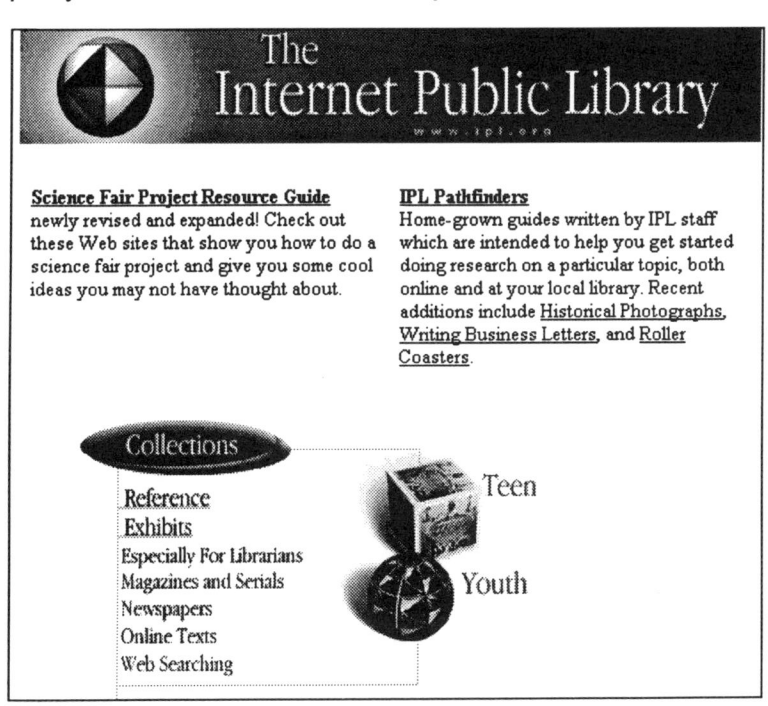

The Internet Public Library

Science Fair Project Resource Guide
newly revised and expanded! Check out these Web sites that show you how to do a science fair project and give you some cool ideas you may not have thought about.

IPL Pathfinders
Home-grown guides written by IPL staff which are intended to help you get started doing research on a particular topic, both online and at your local library. Recent additions include Historical Photographs, Writing Business Letters, and Roller Coasters.

Collections
- Reference
- Exhibits
- Especially For Librarians
- Magazines and Serials
- Newspapers
- Online Texts
- Web Searching

Teen

Youth

The online text area warrants a special mention. Here you can browse by author, title or Dewey Subject Classification (as you would in a real library), and search the text of the books using a simple, yet effective, search interface.

Berkeley Digital Library

The Berkeley Digital Library - http://sunsite.berkeley.edu - is designed to provide access to other online libraries and resources, as well as information and guidance for users who want to create an information resource themselves.

```
                  Berkeley
  Sun SITE        Digital
                  Library
Sun Software, Information & Technology Exchange    SunSITE

The Berkeley Digital Library SunSITE builds digital collections and services while providing information and
support to digital library developers worldwide. We are sponsored by The Library, UC Berkeley and Sun
Microsystems, Inc.

             What's New as of May 17, 2000 8:57 am US Pacific Time
             Site Index | Administration & Policy | Other SunSITEs

The Emma      Catalogs & Indexes              Collections
Goldman Papers Tools for finding what you want. Text and image collections.

              Help/Search                     Information
              Search tools and administrative For digital library developers.
              info.

              Java Corner                     Research & Development
              From our sister SunSITE in      Where digital libraries are being
              Romania.                        built.

              Teaching & Training             Tools
              Resources for lifelong learning. Software for building digital
                                              libraries.
```

It contains links to many other information repositories (including serials, papers and books), and guidance on how to use other search tools to find information online.

Librarians' Index to the Internet

The main page of the Librarians' Index - www.lii.org - to the Internet hosts links to areas such as Geography, Law, Literature, Media, Music, Science and Weather. These main categories are divided into sub-categories, which are also available on the

...Searching the Internet

main Web page, so you can start searching in the right area straight away.
Select a subject area to view and a collection of sites appears, each with a summary of its contents. Unlike major Search Engines, you won't find hundreds of sites in each category - but you can rest assured that the sites listed are well worth visiting.

Encyclopaedia Britannica

Internet users can search the contents of the Encyclopaedia Britannica from its Web site, located at www.britannica.com

The service is free, and also offers a searchable compendium of Web sites and other online resources hand-picked by the Encyclopaedia's editors.

In addition to offering a simple search box, the Encyclopaedia Britannica Web site provides access to a wide range of information resources, including topical information, exhibitions (at the time of writing, there were several interesting exhibitions, including one on health and dinosaurs), multimedia resources, full-length articles and more.

The Library Spot

Just when you think there is way too much information out there for the mere mortal, you stumble across a site like Library Spot - www.libraryspot.com

The wonderful souls who manage this site have put together a collection of premium information resources, ranging from online encyclopaedias to biographical links, calendars, dictionaries, statistics and quotes!

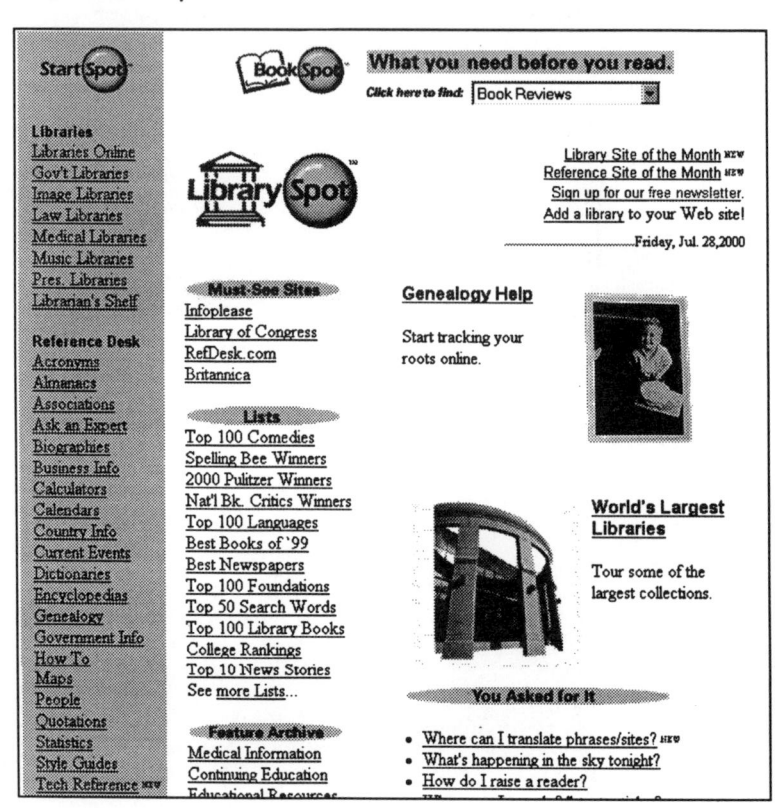

Chapter 16

In Search of the Future

There can be no doubt that Search Engines have made locating information and Web sites easier than ever before. In the space of a few seconds, Internet users can search through tens of millions of pages of information - a task that would take several lifetimes if performed manually.
It doesn't get any better than this. Or does it?

Necessity is the Mother of Invention

Search Engines, for all their power and speed, are inflexible. Users need to spend time learning the nuances of each, coming to grips with any special search requirements that Search Engine requires, and understanding its strengths and weaknesses.

Because of the effort required to master and efficiently use a Search Engine, most Internet users rarely enlist the support of more than one or two. As a result, important Internet resources can remain undiscovered.

Meta-Search Search Engines go some way towards bridging the gap between skilled and novice users, but their interaction with Search Engines is often clumsy, especially when they haven't been updated to reflect new search options and procedures supported by the Search Engines.

Information-hungry users demand a better way.

Intelligent Agents

Intelligent Agent technology, it seems, is the ideal solution. Intelligent Agents can be best thought of as the digital equivalent of exceptionally intelligent and faithful golden retrievers. They are software programs designed to "learn" as much as possible about your interests, your style of expressing yourself and your information requirements.

A typical Intelligent Agent scenario unfolds as follows:

Once installed, the Intelligent Agent program begins to develop a profile of your interests, either by posing a series of questions, or displaying a list of topics for you to rank in order of importance.

The Intelligent Agent then sits back and watches, over your shoulder as it were, as you go about your normal Internet travels. It pays particular attention to the types of Web sites you visit, the Usenet newsgroups you read and the sort of information you access.

Having analysed your information requirements and online habits, the Intelligent Agent is ready to roam the Internet in search of useful titbits of information and other resources. Every now and then it will send you an email message summarising its latest findings, listing the sites it has visited and the information they contain and noting why it thinks you will find them useful.

The Future Today

Sound too sci-fi to believe? Well, you're right - at least in part.

Intelligent Agents have been with us for several years now, and have only recently begun to approach the level of sophistication described above. Although current versions demonstrate certain levels of autonomy and "artificial intelligence", we are still several years away from personalised, independent information agents.

However, some of today's Intelligent Agents are a useful addition to your information-searching tool chest. They will, for example, scour Search Engines and other online directories, looking for sites relevant to your search queries (although they still rely greatly on your involvement, both in deciding where to look and what to look for). But, correctly implemented, these programs are both fun to use and offer powerful search functions.

Unfortunately, interest in creating personal Intelligent Agents is waning, as companies realise the difficulties of developing profitable business models for such software.

Most Intelligent Agent research is now focused on applications to electronic commerce - for example, developing agents that learn your taste in music, books and entertainment and scan the Net looking for the best deals on your behalf.

Such online shopping agents can save you time and money. They will compare the prices advertised online for a specific product or service, then ensure you get the best price. Try the agents below:

Even Better	www.evenbetter.com
mySimon	www.mysimon.com
R U SURE	www.rusure.com
PriceScan	www.pricescan.com
BottomDollar	www.bottomdollar.com

Collaborative Filtering

When you're interested in checking out a new movie, or buying a book or CD, you generally ask friends for recommendations, or create a shortlist and seek feedback from others on which they consider the best.

Collaborative filtering services work in a similar way. For example, a collaborative filtering agent may note your preferences for books. It would then compare your preferences against its database of other people's preferences, and provide recommendations on the basis of what other purchasers with similar tastes have bought. As you share common tastes and interests, the recommendations are likely to be accurate.

While this technology is especially useful to match recommendations for consumer goods, such as films, books, videos, music, holidays and wine, it can also be used to help refine Internet searches.

For instance, if a Search Engine could track Web resources accessed by other users looking for the same information as you, it could provide you with a useful list of sites. In addition, it could personalise this list on the basis of which sites were selected by those searchers as being the most relevant.

There are a number of examples of collaborative filtering at work.

Amazon (www.amazon.com), the online book, video and music store, keeps track of your purchases, and each time you return to the site, recommends similar items. If Amazon is spot-on with its recommendations, you can leave the system as is. Otherwise, you can finetune its recommendations.

Alexa (www.alexa.com) works in a similar manner, but deals with searches. Once downloaded and installed, the Alexa client software monitors your Web searches and suggests other resources based on its database of resources chosen by users with similar interests. It also automatically recommends Web sites related to the content of the site or page you are viewing. Alexa technology has now been integrated into the latest versions of Microsoft's Internet Explorer and the Netscape Web browser.

For further examples of this kind of technology at work, see:
Movie Critic   www.moviecritic.com
Cyberian Outpost   www.outpost.com
Virtual Vineyards   www.virtualvin.com

Virtual Personalities

Virtual personality technology is often shown in movies in which a user asks a computer a question using natural language and the computer responds in kind within seconds.

Many businesses, such as vendors and service providers, deal with hundreds or thousands of customer queries each day. Most of these queries are handled by call centres, staffed by people who manually research customer questions and provide answers as fast as possible (preferably while the customer is on the telephone).

As you can imagine, the investment in both staff and technology in call centres is large. Therefore, such businesses are turning to "artificial intelligence" technology in an effort to find a cost-efficient alternative.

There have been many successful demonstrations of artificially intelligent software bots capable of carrying on a conversation with users and interpreting and answering questions. Undoubtedly, we will see more of this technology in the near future.

For instance, instead of calling Microsoft's technical support helpline, you will visit its Web site and submit details of your problem to its Help Agent. The agent will try to troubleshoot your problem, guiding you through various software configuration issues and advising you of possible conflicts. If it cannot resolve the problem, you will be directed to the person best qualified to address the issue.

In the not-too-distant future, when high-speed Internet access is widespread, it is likely you will speak to the Help Agent using Internet telephony-style technology (here you speak into your computer's microphone and hear responses via the speakers). Help Agents will respond in your preferred language, with perfect grammar, sentence construction and vocal inflections - in fact, it will be hard to tell the difference between a human operator and a Help Agent (except, perhaps, that the software agent won't lose its patience!).

Curious about the possibilities of this technology? Visit the sites listed below:
Virtual Personalities   www.vperson.com
eGain Assistant   www.egain.com
Neuromedia   www.neuromedia.com

A number of "natural language AI agents" agents are already available to play and experiment with. These are designed to recognise your questions and comments, and reply in a realistic fashion.

To get an idea of how far research in artificial intelligence has progressed, why not initiate a conversation with one?
Brain the Bot   orlo.emi.net/html/brainframe.htm
Chat to Mabel   www.hamill.co.uk/mabel/
ALICE   birch.eecs.lehigh.edu/alice/

The Best of All Worlds
It won't be long before the next generation of Search Engines benefits from a convergence of these technologies, making online searching similar to being guided through the vast resources of the Internet by a digital librarian.

Imagine you need to obtain a chemical analysis of Moon dust. Not being a geologist or chemist, you have no idea where to start. So you fire up your computer, log onto the Internet and visit your favourite Search Engine.

You are greeted by the smiling face of Jackie, your personalised Search Agent (you designed her to remind you of the friendly librarian who helped you with your Grade 5 English essay). You speak into the microphone built into your computer monitor:

"Jackie, I need some help. Do you know where I can find a chemical breakdown of Moon dust?"

The Net-Works Guide to...

Jackie furrows her brow (she is, after all, programmed to replicate human emotions).

"You mean an analysis of the dust astronauts brought back from the Moon?", she replies.

"Yes!", you say, smiling.

"Do you want me to tell you the answer, or would you like some pointers?", Jackie asks.

"Just some pointers, thanks. I guess I should work it out for myself", you reply.

Your screen fills with links to various research papers and online science journals, each neatly summarised (so that's what Jackie gets up to in her spare time!).

Not a bad future, if you ask me!

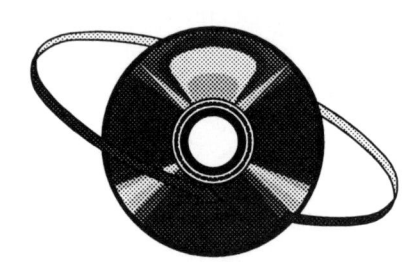

Appendix

Search Engines and Software

There are hundreds of excellent Search Engines on the Internet. Unfortunately, this guide has only been able to canvass a handful. Below is a partial list of other Search Engines - some well known, others not - that you might like to explore for yourself.

Search Engines

Magellan	magellan.excite.com
BusinessWeb	www.businesswebsource.com
What-U-Seek	whatuseek.com
Fast Search	www.alltheweb.com
Galaxy	www.einet.net
Starting Point	www.stpt.com
Look Smart	www.looksmart.com
Matilda Search Engine	www.aaa.com.au
Nerd World	www.nerdworld.com
Web Wombat	www.webwombat.com.au
The Argus Clearinghouse	www.clearinghouse.net
Searches	www.searches.com
Northern Light	www.northernlight.com
One Seek	www.oneseek.com

Other Meta-Search Search Engines

All-in-One	www.allonesearch.com
CINet Search	search.cnet.com
SavvySearch	www.savvysearch.com
SearchBug	www.searchbug.com
PureSearch	www.puresearch.com
Debriefing	www.debriefing.com
MatchSite	www.matchsite.com

Chubba	www.chubba.com
Black Widow	www.widow.com
Supercrawler	www.supercrawler.com

Search and Agent Software

Below is a list of Search and Agent programs to download and play with.

Copernic 2000	www.copernic.com
WebFerret	www.ferretsoft.com
Bulls Eye	www.intelliseek.com
Mata Hari	www.thewebtools.com
Search Wolf	www.trellian.com/search/
QueryN MetaSearch	www.queryn.com
Net Attache	www.tympani.com
Top 10 Tracker	www.top-10.com
Digout4U	www.arisem.com
WebSeeker	www.bluesquirrel.com
GuruNet	www.gurunet.com
FlySwat	www.flyswat.com

Search Engine Companion Programs

A number of Web Search Engines offer customised software that allows you to perform searches without running your Web browser. This can decrease search times, as you don't need to wait for images and other extras to download.

The list below contains several such programs.

InfoSeek QuickSeek

Works with both Internet Explorer and Netscape Navigator/Communicator, allowing you to search InfoSeek without first connecting to the site. Get your copy (PC or Mac) from:

www.infoseek.com/iseek?pg=quickseek/Download.html

InfoSeek Desktop

Search InfoSeek directly from your desktop, without a Web browser:

www.infoseek.com/iseek?pg=desktop/Download.html

Excite Direct
This Web browser add-on allows you to submit searches from within your favourite browser. To find out more visit:
   www.excite.com/direct/excite_direct.htmlG

Webopedia Search Tool   webopedia.com/searchtool/
AltaVista Discovery   discovery.altavista.com
Lycos SeeMore   www.lycos.com/seemore/
Yahoo! Companion
   edit.yahoo.com/config/download_companion

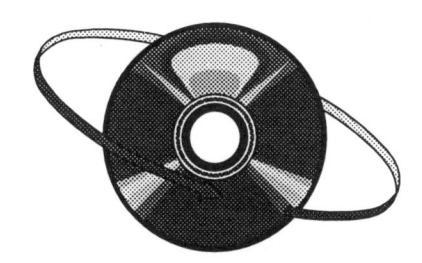

The Net-Works Guide to...

Glossary

account
Before you can access the Internet, you need an account on a computer connected to the Internet. Your Internet Service Provider will provide you with an account. The name of your account becomes your userid.

Agent
An Agent, also known as an Intelligent Agent, is a software program designed to search the Internet for information on behalf of its owner.

anonymous ftp
The process of connecting to other computers on the Internet which allow public access (that is, which don't require you to have an account before you connect) in order to retrieve files stored on them. Connection is established using the ftp program, logging in with the username anonymous and entering your email address as the password.

Archie
A service used to search for files or directories on computers on the Internet which allow anonymous ftp logins. Once you locate the file, you can download it using your Web browser or an ftp program.

ARPANet
The origin of the global network now called the Internet. In the 1960s ARPANet was created for the US military, which has since developed its own network called MILNet.

article
A message posted on the Usenet news system.

ASCII
American Standard Code for Information Interchange. The main printable character set used by today's computers.

binary file
A computer file which contains characters other than pure (ascii) text.

bit
A concatenation of binary digit. The smallest unit of measure-ment of computer data.

Boolean
Boolean operators, AND, NOT and OR, are used to refine search queries by telling Search Engines how to treat or match search terms.

bps
Bits per second. The speed by which modems are rated. This specifies the amount of data they can send and receive each second.

byte
A byte is made up of (usually) eight bits. A byte is the smallest addressable unit of data storage. A kilobyte is a thousand bytes, a megabyte is a thousand thousand bytes.

client
A software program that connects to and inter-

...Searching the Internet

acts with another computer resource (called a server program). In Internet terms, a client program is a program that interacts with an Internet resource, such as a Web site or Gopher site.

dial-up
(1) The act of temporarily connecting to another computer using a modem and an ordinary telephone line (2) A type of account on a Unix host which allows limited access to its services (usually accessed via temporary modem connection).

DNS Domain Name System. The system that regulates the naming of computers on the Internet.The name and network address of every computer connected to the Internet is stored in a massive database which other computers access in order to translate computer names (such as domain.com.uk) to numeric (IP) addresses (like 123.321.43.34).

domain name
The official name for a computer connected to the Internet. Your email address is comprised of your userid and the domain name of your ISP's computer, separated by @ i.e. userid@name.

download
The act of copying files from one computer (referred to as a remote host) to your computer.

dumb terminal
In essence a computer screen and keyboard, connected by cable to a central computer. It is called a "dumb" terminal because it lacks storage space (i.e. a hard disk) and a CPU.

email
Electronic mail - electronic correspondence sent from one computer to another over a network.

email address
Your email address contains all the information other computers connected to the Internet need to deliver email to you. It is comprised of your userid and the domain name of your ISP's com-puter, separated by the @ symbol; i.e. userid@domainname.

FAQ Frequently Asked Questions.
A FAQ file is a compilation of questions and answers, designed to help newcomers to the Net.

finger
A program that allows you to determine if users are logged on, plus other useful information about them (such as when they were last logged on and whether they have any unread email).

followup
A reply to a Usenet posting which can be read by other Usenet readers. Newsreaders allow you to either reply directly to the author of an article (by email), or post your reply to the newsgroup for other subscribers to read.

ftp
(1) The file transfer protocol - the standard that dictates the manner in which files are copied from computer to computer across the Internet (2) The program used to copy files from one computer to another across the Internet.

The Net-Works Guide to...

Gopher
A menu-driven interface used to find information on different computer systems. Usually accessed via telnet or a gopher client.

Host
A computer on the Internet that allows users to connect to it.

http hypertext transfer protocol
The protocol that regulates how information is transferred over the World Wide Web. Hyper-text forms the basis of the World Wide Web.

Internet Service Provider (ISP)
A company that provides Internet access.

InterNIC
The Internet Network Information Centre, the closest thing to a central organising body.

Internet Protocol (IP)
One of the many protocols or standards that regulate the way in which information is passed between computers on the Internet.

mailing list
A list of email addresses of people who share an interest. When you send an email message via a mailing list it is automatically copied and sent to every other person on that list.

modem
A device used to connect two computers via a telephone line.

moderator
The person who scrutinises posts made to moderated newsgroups to ensure that they are accurate and on topic.

MUD Multi-User Dungeon.
Text-based online fantasy worlds, where one can fight dragons and mythical creatures.

newsgroup
The electronic notice or bulletin boards that comprise Usenet.

newsreader
A program used to read, post or reply to news articles on Usenet.

packet
A unit of data sent over a network.

password
A secret word or code used, together with your userid, to connect to your account, or to another computer on the Internet.

PPP See SLIP/PPP.

protocol
A standard that dictates how computers on a network interact with each other. The most important protocol for Internet computers is TCP/IP.

Query
A query, commonly referred to as a search query (or search parameter), is one or more words submitted to a Search Engine or similar resource to define the information for which you are looking.

...Searching the Internet

router
A device that transfers data between one or more networks, ensuring that it is delivered quickly and efficiently.

server
(1) Software used to provide access to an Inter-net resource e.g. a Gopher Server. To access the server software, you usually need a client program.
(2) The computer running the server software.

Search Engine
A Web site designed primarily to keep track of other Web sites. Search Engines, with the assistance of Web Robot programs, explore and index Web sites.

SLIP/PPP
Serial Line Internet Protocol/Point-to-Point. Two different types of software used to connect computers via modem. When you run either SLIP or PPP software on your computer to connect to your ISP's computer, you are assigned an IP address, and become a part of the Internet for the duration of that connection.

TCP
Transmission Control Protocol. A protocol or standard that regulates how information is shared between computers on a network.

telnet
A program used to connect to computers over the Internet.

Usenet
The collection of thousands of electronic noticeboards or discussion groups where information and ideas are exchanged on an endless array of topics.

upload
The act of sending files or any piece of information from your computer to another computer, usually referred to as a remote host.

Web Robot
A Web Robot, also known as a spider or craw-ler program, is a software program that explores and downloads the contents of individual Web pages in order to categorise and index them. Web robots are used by Search Engines to keep their databases up to date.

World Wide Web (WWW)
A hypertext-based system linking information and files on different computers on the Internet. One of the most recent developments on the Internet, it allows users to browse information using an intuitive graphical user interface (GUI).

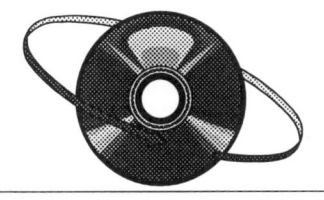

The Net-Works Guide to...

The Net-Works Guide to
Creating a Website

This book, written by a Website design and marketing consultant, won't drown the reader in jargon, or skip over the important issues.

How to research and plan your site; What free tools are available that make producing your own Web site child's play;

How to create your own dazzling graphics, using a variety of cheap or free computer graphics programs;

Who to talk to when it comes to finding a home for your Web site (If you have an Internet account, you probably already have all that you need);

How to put it all together and achieve a great look with a minimum of fuss, and

How to advertise your Web site and attract other Internet users to it.

Tim Ireland   128 pages   £6.95

The Net-Works Guide to
Marketing Your Website

How to get visitors to your website.

Simply creating a website and putting it on the Internet is not enough to generate online sales. In Cyberspace there simply isn't any passing traffic. The customer is king, and they will selectively choose which sites they are going to visit. Indeed, without a well thought out and successfully implemented marketing plan, the majority will not even know that you are out there.

The Net-Works Guide to Marketing Your Website will show you how to construct and deliver a successful promotional strategy.

Tim Ireland   128 pages   £7.95

The Internet for Managers

Many managers still view the Internet as a scary place. It appears to be the preserve of the technical wizard and even the acronyms seem incomprehensible. *The Internet for Managers* tackles this problem head on and gives all levels of management enough information to 'hold their own' in meetings and to take on board the issues which affect their spheres of responsibility. It explains all the key concepts from the basics of Web browsing through to the establishment of corporate security policies in clear, non-technical terms.

Learn about: Joining the Net... Constructing Websites... Electronic Trading... Marketing Online... Intranets, Teleworking and the Virtual Corporation... Technical Issues... Security Problems... Language Difficulties... Legal Implications... and much more.

RRC Penfold   192 pages   £12.95

Starting and Running a Business on the Internet

In 1995, businesses clocked up more than £300 million in sales over the Internet. Within five years that figure had risen to over £20 billion and is still growing almost exponentially!

These cyber-businesses use the Internet to slash costs; improve their customer relations and support; sell their products direct to the customer; cut marketing expenses and to reach hitherto untapped markets. Their secrets are revealed in this book, so that British business can make money on the Internet before their competitors beat them to it.

Alex Kiam   112 pages   £6.95

Book Ordering

To order any of these books, please order from our secure website at **www.net-works.co.uk** or complete the form below (or use a plain piece of paper) and send to:

Europe/Asia
TTL, PO Box 200, Harrogate HG1 2YR, England (or fax to 01423-526035, or email: sales@net-works.co.uk).

USA/Canada
Trafalgar Square, PO Box 257, Howe Hill Road, North Pomfret, Vermont 05053 (or fax to 802-457-1913, call toll free 800-423-4525, or email: tsquare@sover.net)

Postage and handling charge:
UK - £1 for first book, and 50p for each additional book
USA - $5 for first book, and $2 for each additional book (all shipments by UPS, please provide street address).
Elsewhere - £3 for first book, and £1.50 for each additional book via surface post (for airmail and courier rates, please fax or email for a price quote)

Book	Qty	Price
	Postage	
	Total:	

☐ I enclose payment for £_____
☐ Please debit my VISA/AMEX/MASTERCARD

Number: ☐☐☐☐ ☐☐☐☐ ☐☐☐☐ ☐☐☐☐
Expiry Date: ☐☐☐☐ Signature: _____ Date: _____

Name: _____
Address: _____
_____
_____
Postcode/Zip: _____
Telephone/Email: _____

Searchint